SEEING PAST THE STORM

ANDREA JOYCE

Copyright © 2021 by Andrea Joyce

All rights reserved. All rights reserved. No part of this book may be reproduced in any form or by any means without the prior written consent of the Publisher, excepting brief quotes used in reviews.

ISBN: 9798502207881

Edited by: Eutopia Nicole

Book Cover Design by: Eutopia Nicole

Painting by: Eutopia Nicole

FOREWORD

It's been said that a child's first best friend is their cousin. The statement rings true with me and Andrea Joyce. My cousin and I have been sibling close bonded tighter than our childhood braids for as long as I can remember. When you're this close to someone, you learn to trust each other with your hopes, dreams, and fears.

As children, we fantasized about how life in the future would be for us. We'd continue through school, find the perfect spouses, and raise our children to be as close as we vowed to always remain. That was probably the only aspect we could control. We remained close throughout the trials of adolescence and the excitement of our budding adulthoods. We supported each other through the many milestones in our lives. She's one of the few people I speak to daily.

As I read through the pages, they transported me back to many of the events of the past; marriages and divorces, births and deaths were all family affairs. My cousin dug much deeper than these already tough times. She reveals personal hurts, violations, and betrayals and when you're mad enough to fight, she shows you how love and forgiveness can transform your life.

Andrea Joyce is one of the most compassionate, loving and encouraging people you will ever meet. She is uniquely complex and multi-faceted like a rare diamond, and like diamonds, pressure and force created a masterpiece. She is one of my loudest, most consistent cheerleaders. Andrea is always ready to soothe any situation with a joke and a prayer.

In Seeing Past the Storm, Andrea takes you through the storms that meant to destroy her life. Her ability to tell her story and make you feel her pain allows you, as a reader, to release your own pain. The candid ownership of the role she played in her storms proves we can evaluate ourselves with sincerity and learn from the events of our lives. We can move past the clouded visions in our storms into the presence of who we would be. Andrea Joyce doesn't just tell us what happened in her life, she provides a pathway to healing.

Eutopia Nicole
Author

Andrea Joyce

To my three heartbeats, my children, Icis, DeAngelo and Danielle, who have weathered the storms with me. I love you.

ACKNOWLEDGMENTS

July 2021

I would first like to thank God for the strength to write this story. Thank You, Father, for each and every blessing You bestow upon me. Thank You for Your healing and restoration power. With You I can do all things. I will never have enough words to tell You how grateful I am to You. I love You Father.

With much appreciation to:

My mother, Marjorie Cameron, this story is as much yours as it is mine. I would not have a story to tell if you had not decided one day to have me. Though there have been some rough patches, I am so grateful that we were able to overcome them. There is nothing like a mother's love. Thank you for loving me through all my mess. I am grateful and humbled by your unconditional love. Thank you for never giving up on me. I love you.

My biological father, James Carr, it is because of who you were that I am who I am today. I am grateful to you, and I love you. Rest in Heavenly peace.

My dad, Daniel Cameron, you took an unlovable girl and loved her through her hurt and pain. You loved me so much I had no choice but to love you, too. I wish we had more time together; however, I am grateful for the time we had. Thank you for loving my mother, marrying her, and bringing me into the Cameron family. Thank you for showing me what genuine love looked like. I hope to one day have a man love me as much or more than you did and treat me as well. You are my inspiration. I love you Daddy and I miss you like crazy. Rest in Heavenly peace.

My aunt, Phyllis Bryant, you were my second mom and the person who gave me so much love when I needed it. I was your "Peach", and I am forever grateful to you. You taught me to laugh at life and embrace my silliness. Thank you for teaching me to bake. I use it as a way to relieve stress. I miss sitting on your knee and telling you my secrets. I still dial your number, wishing I could speak with you. I love and miss you. Rest in Heaven.

My Carr, Cameron and Stradford family, my siblings, aunts and uncles, cousins, nieces, and nephews, thank you for your love and support throughout the years. I have the best family. I love you.

Andrea Joyce

My couster, thank you. Thank you for believing in me since I was a child. Thank you for always supporting and pushing me. Thank you for designing the cover, editing the book, and writing the Foreword. I appreciate you so much. You are a star Eutopia Nicole, and I am blessed that you love me unconditionally. I am so excited about the books you are writing; you are going to be a best-selling author! You were my first real friend and are still my best friend. I love you cousin!

My Coach, Titanya "Ty" Johnson aka Lady Ty the Great, thank you. One phone conversation with you turned into one of the best things I have ever done, releasing my testimonies. Writing this book has helped me "clean out the closet" on some hurts I did not know I still had. This is more than a book to me; it is my healing process. I appreciate you for being obedient to God by first writing your book *Daddy Issues* and then creating the writing groups. Your obedience allowed me to write books. You have helped dozens of people write and self-publish their books and you will soon help hundreds of thousands. Thank you for pushing me to write this book and to find my authentic voice. You are true blue, and I appreciate you!

To the T.O.T.s and the Greats, you have become my family. What a blessing to have you all in my life. Thank you for your time, encouragement, love, prayers, and your friendship. You are all brilliant authors with grand stories to tell. Keep writing and keep elevating to your Zone of Genius. You were made to fly!

And finally, to all my readers, for purchasing this book. I hope in some way it blesses you and helps you overcome any storms you may be facing. I thank you for your current and continued support.

Also, I would love to hear from you. When you get the chance, please email me at authorandreajoyce@gmail.com or visit my website at www.authorandreajoyce.com.

Thank you and blessings always,

Andrea Joyce

TABLE OF CONTENTS

I. THE STORMS   8

Chapter 1	The Storm: Abandonment	10
Chapter 2	The Storm: Rejection	16
Chapter 3	The Storm: Violation	20
Chapter 4	The Storm: Heartbreak	28
Chapter 5	The Storm: Betrayal	39
Chapter 6	The Storm: Homelessness	47
Chapter 7	The Storm: Addiction	53
Chapter 8	The Storm: Suicide	58
Chapter 9	The Storm: Depression	65

II. SEEING PAST THE STORM   70

Chapter 10	Seeing Past Abandonment	73
Chapter 11	Seeing Past Rejection	78
Chapter 12	Seeing Past Violation	81
Chapter 13	Seeing Past Heartbreak	84
Chapter 14	Seeing Past Betrayal	87
Chapter 15	Seeing Past Homelessness	90
Chapter 16	Seeing Past Addiction	93
Chapter 17	Seeing Past Suicide	97
Chapter 18	Seeing Past Depression	100

III. THE BLESSING IN THE STORM   103

IV. WORDS FROM THE AUTHOR   108

V. ABOUT THE AUTHOR   110

I. THE STORMS

THE STORMS

"If you do not deal with turmoil, you cannot heal from it."

Andrea Joyce

24 "Therefore whoever hears these sayings of Mine, and does them, I will liken him to a wise man who built his house on the rock: 25 and the rain descended, the floods came, and the winds blew and beat on that house; and it did not fall, for it was founded on the rock.

26 "But everyone who hears these sayings of Mine, and does not do them, will be like a foolish man who built his house on the sand: 27 and the rain descended, the floods came, and the winds blew and beat on that house; and it fell. And great was its fall." Matthew 7:24-27 (NKJV)

Andrea Joyce

The Storm: Abandonment

"When my father and my mother forsake me,
Then the Lord will take care of me." Psalm 27:10 (NKJV)

SEEING PAST THE STORM

A girl's first love is her father.

I was a daddy's girl from birth. I have always been told I look and act just like my father. Maybe that is why I was always trying to be with him; I never wanted to leave his side. One of the first memories of my father was me drinking hot chocolate out of my new McDonald's mug, the one with the smiley face on it. I was 4 years old. Breakfast was on the table and my parents were laughing. There was music playing. Everything was wonderful.

One morning while I was sitting on his lap and drinking out of my mug, I heard a loud noise, and my mug went flying. It shattered. I jumped off my father's lap, crying and yelling about my mug, noticing nothing but the broken pieces. I remember gathering the shards. Since that day, I have been trying to put the broken pieces of my life back together. That morning a storm began rising, and it was a storm that would forever change my life. This storm would become abandonment, and the man I loved with all my heart, my first love, my father, would be the cause.

In my child's mind, my parents separated and divorced in a matter of minutes. I was not sure of what was happening around me, but by the time I was 5 years old, my father no longer lived in our home. Sometimes he would call, and I'd ask him to come back, but he never did. None of my tears could move my father back home.

By the time I was 7, Mom had remarried, had another child, and moved us into a new home. Life was moving along at breakneck speed. Even though the changes were good, I still pined for my father to come back home.

Eventually, my biological father began calling me and making dates to take me out. I would run around putting together outfits for our big dates. I skipped through the house, hurrying to complete my chores. The mornings of our dates the sun always seemed to shine brighter, the sky was bluer, and the birds chirped louder. Our dates were magical. Sometimes he would take me to see a Broadway play. The hum of the curtains moving back, the anticipation in the air as we waited for the first words or first song to be revealed, or just having my biological father there, engraved a love of stage plays into my heart. Other times we would hang out in Times Square. The lights of the signs and stores were breathtaking. I would feel the heartbeat of the city and knew I would forever be a city girl. There were times we'd do regular things like go clothes shopping or out to eat but being with my father made them much more than regular everyday experiences. My favorite dates with him were going out to diners. Diners were our favorite places to eat. In a world before beepers and cell phones, I had his undivided attention. He would be focused on me and me only. I lived for those moments. What I did not live for were his broken promises. My father was good at making plans. He was not the best at following through on them. There were many times he would plan an event for us, and it would not happen. I would tell my friends I could not play outside that day because my dad was coming. Chores were done with lightning speed. I would get dressed in some cute outfit and wait by the window for his car to pull up. I did not always know what car to look for because my father changed cars like people changed underwear. As soon as I would hear a car coming down our block, I would sit up in anticipation, wondering if it was him. The disappointment I felt when the car continued down the street was heartbreaking until another car would drive down. Minutes became hours, with no father in sight. I would keep hoping though. I would not move from the window until night fell, and my mother coaxed me to go take my bath and eat. My tears soaked my pillow, but every time he called, I would get excited and believe that the next time he would show up like he had promised.

When my father did not show up, he would give me a sizable amount of money or buy the latest fad that was out to make up for his absence. Yes, I had looked good, but I felt terrible and had a hole in my heart that his gifts could never fill. I acted out in school and at home because I knew that if I got into trouble, my mother would call my father and he would have come over. I talked back, rebelled, was a class clown and became a problem child. Teachers could not keep me quiet, no matter how many threats of calling my parents they gave. That is what I wanted, for my father to show up. And he did fuss at me, threaten to punish me, he even spanked me once, but he showed up, so my mission was accomplished.

Hatred began brewing in my heart. I hated my biological father did not live with us, hated that there was another man taking his place and hated that my mom would not take him back. This hatred stemmed from conversations my father and I would have. He would tell me he wanted to come back home, that he wanted to be back with my mother, but because of my stepfather he was not able to. He would tell me that if her husband were not in the picture, my mother would take him back and we could be a family again. When he called, he would often ask about my mother, how she was doing, what she was doing. Was she still with that man? It was very awkward for me. It caused me to resent my stepfather. If he was not there, then my father could be. So, I started acting out. I directed my anger and resentment at my stepfather and was disrespectful to him. I tried to avoid him by staying in my room. In the corner of my room, while reading or playing with my dolls, I fantasized about him leaving and my father coming back. I tried to plan ways to break up my mother's marriage. My plan was for them to argue then she would get mad at him like she did with my father and then they would divorce, too. My father told me he still loved my mother and wanted another chance. I wanted that breakfast and music feeling back, and I felt like I was caught in the middle between my first love and my new family.

My father had many games for my young mind. For years, he told me not to call my mother's husband "dad". I felt guilty. I did not want to anger my father, but my stepfather treated me like his daughter, and I wanted to call him dad. I only called him dad out of the earshot of my father. I became adept at when I could and could not call my stepfather, dad. I remember asking my mother if she could change my last name to theirs since I was the only one living in our house with a different last name. I wanted to belong. I wanted to have a normal family life like my friends. They had a mother and a father in the home, and they all had the same last name; no one looked at them as if they were strange. My mother asked my biological father if she could change my last name, but he shot her down. This made me furious because I felt he was punishing me because regular families all had the same last name. I tired of my teachers and classmates getting my mother's last name wrong then looking at me like some kind of freak because our names did not match. To this day, though I am divorced, I kept my married name for my children.

For years, my biological father tried to disrupt, shake up, and cause friction within my home. My father tried to shake up our family and cause friction between me and my dad for years. My mother never condemned him, even encouraging me to reach out, as he became more and more absent in my life. "Have you called your father?" became her weekly mantra. I would sigh, pick up the phone, dial his number and leave a message. He would not call back for weeks, sometimes months at a time. By the time I was 16 years old, I had had enough. I was tired of begging him for his time. After all, he was the adult, wasn't it his job to be the parent and reach out to me? Besides my unanswered and unreturned calls, I became weary of having to share his attention when he came around. When he showed up, he started bringing women on our father-daughter dates. To this day, I am not sure if he was showing me off to them or trying to get their approval of me, but every time he showed up to pick me up, he either had a woman in the car or there was one waiting at the location when we arrived. They would try to butter me up and I would laugh on the inside because I knew being nice to me would not get them an in with him. Being nice to me would not win them any points with him because he was rarely in my life, my approval or disapproval of them did not matter. The more missing in action he became, the closer my stepfather, who was now just dad, and I became. My dad went to my school and church events, he would tell me about his growing up, and he encouraged me to be whatever I wanted to be. His time, unbroken promises and unconditional love helped me feel welcomed into the Cameron family. It also helped me move past not having my biological father's attention. My stepfather became my real dad and moved into first place in my heart. I never characterized him as a stepfather, he was truly my dad. Most people never knew he was not my biological father, and that suited us just fine. Even if my last name was not the same as his, I was his daughter and I was accepted. With this sense of approval, I decided I was done with begging for scraps of my biological father's attention. I stopped reaching out to him. I avoided his calls, and he ceased to exist to me for years.

My mother tried to tell me for years to forgive my biological father. Instead, I went through my teens and early adulthood with repressed feelings of resentment, hatred, anger, neglect, and abandonment. Those negative emotions shaped my personal and professional relationships. I stumbled into unhealthy friendships and associations and gravitated toward males that unconsciously reminded me of my father. I began seeking validation and unconditional love from every person I encountered. For a large part of my life, I was miserable, even though I smiled and laughed. I didn't know how to get past the negative emotions that threatened to destroy me. If I wanted to be free from negativity, there was one thing I needed to learn.

I had to learn how to forgive.

Andrea Joyce

The Storm: Rejection

"He came to that which was his own,
but his own did not receive him." John 1:11 (NIV)

"I don't date black girls."

I looked up into the face of the boy I had been crushing on since fifth grade. My eyebrows squished together as I gazed at him with my head tilted. I did not understand how this black boy did not like black girls. When we met, black girls surrounded him. He was at the park playing basketball with his friends. He had no shortage of admirers because he was the cutest boy on the court. His curly black hair and dimples made him stand out. After the game, our eyes met, but we never spoke. It surprised me to run into him at the library a few days later. He walked up to me, introduced himself and we were friends ever since. We were in 8th grade; I attended catholic school, and he attended public school. He would pass by my school every day. Over the years we would walk home together sometimes, talking about everything. I had finally worked up my nerve to tell him I thought he was cute.

He continued, "I think you're pretty, you're smart, nice, and funny. You have a nice body. I like all of that, but I just don't date black girls."

Words tumbled from my mouth, "but you're black." I didn't understand how I had all the qualities he liked, but he would not date me because I was African American.

He explained, "no you're black, you know dark. I don't date dark skinned girls." And then he walked off, taking my self-esteem with him.

My skin tone was still causing me problems. All during elementary school I had suffered teasing by classmates and friends because I was dark skinned. I was called everything from tar baby, to blackie to midnight. It hurt, but I had learned to retaliate. I would talk about the person first before they could talk about me and have everyone laugh at them. It had been working, but now a boy I had liked and been friends with for three years had dropped a grenade on my heart and it exploded. If I were lighter, he would have dated me. I cursed my dark skin yet again.

It was not like I hadn't tried to get rid of my dark skin. My aunt bought me skin bleaching creams I tried. I rubbed them into my skin twice a day, with no success. I tried staying out of the sun as recommended, but I missed playing outside with my friends. I tried wearing sun visors and hats, but it was too hot. Walking under umbrellas to avoid the sun was too much work.

That day I was desperate and tried something different. When I got home, I ran a bath with hot water and got the bleach from the laundry room. I poured half the bottle into the tub and waited for the water to rise. I was going to use real bleach to bleach the black out of my skin so I could be lighter. I wanted to be accepted by him and those that teased me. I hoped I would finally shed the dark skin that plagued me.

As the water rose the smell of the bleach became more pungent, and my stomach revolted, making me nauseous. I could not put myself into that water, no matter how hard I tried. I turned off the water, draining the tub. Tears flowed down my face as the water spun around and down the drain. I realized I would never be rid of my dark skin. The emotional toll still weighs on me so many years later, the smell of bleach makes me gag.

Cruel teasing and rejection were not the only times I hated my skin. There were times I'd want to wear a bright color and was told that I was too dark to wear it or if I put on a bright lipstick or lip gloss shade, I was told that I looked like a horse's ass. As time went on, I believed the things that were said to me and said about me. I began wearing only dark clothes; black and gray were my colors of choice. I thought they would help camouflage me. I continued using the bleaching creams and scrubbing my skin extra hard in the tub, trying to rid of the cursed dark skin. If I were around people and it was dark, I would ask them to turn the lights on; I had been teased by people saying I was so dark they could not see me at night or without light. Though I stared at red-, yellow- and orange-colored items, I said green was my favorite color because it was unobtrusive. The only time I wore bright colors was on my nails because they were only an extension of me; they would not be too bright for my face.

For years I carried around the negative feelings of rejection, low self-esteem, and self-hatred.

I had to learn how to love the skin I was in.

Andrea Joyce

The Storm: Violation

"This is what the Lord says:
'Cursed is the man who trusts in mankind
And makes flesh his [a]strength,'" Jeremiah 17:5 (NASB)

It's devastating when the one you trust turns on you.

In 1990, I thought I would rule the world. I planned my life. I was going to college and would graduate with a political science degree. Then I would go to law school and matriculate with a juris doctorate in criminal law. I would be married by the age of 25 and have two children, a boy and a girl, a nice Pekingese or Yorkie and live in a 4-bedroom, 3-bathroom gated home.

Funny how the best laid plans turn topsy turvy with one incident. As I crossed the stage for my high school graduation, I looked out and smiled at the plans I had made for my life. Graduation, check. Now it was time to go to college. I had registered for my first semester classes, said goodbye to my family and met my best friends, all on the first day of college. My high school sweetheart and I had broken up, so I was ready to enjoy the single life with my girls. We were 17 and ready for fun. We could be found in each other's dorm rooms or at parties on and off campus. During one of our adventures, we met a group of boys that were best friends. We hung out a few times and then began dating them. We were inseparable. Where you saw one couple, you saw the other two. Our friend circle was large. It included the friends we had before we became couples. As freshman, we could not have cars on campus, and we were fortunate to have friends with cars. We were also fortunate to have friends with apartments and trailers off campus. We would hang out, cook, listen to music, and party off campus often. One night, after having missed dinner in the cafeteria, one of my best friends and I went to a restaurant off campus for pancakes and eggs. While walking there, we discussed our weekend plans and a male friend of ours pulled up. He asked where we were going and if we wanted a ride there. We agreed, hopped into his car, and headed to the restaurant. After ordering he asked if we wanted to hang out with him for a little while; he had gotten in some new rap cassette tapes and wanted us to listen to them. I had been wanting to hear the new Yo-Yo album, so we agreed to hang out with him. I was excited to hear new music from a west coast female rapper. We got to his place and walked in. Walking through his front door, I noticed that there was a guy there that I had never met. He introduced us and then suggested we eat. After eating and talking, he suggested I follow him to his room so I could listen to the new music. Since he had a high-tech audio system in his bedroom, it wasn't unusual for us to go in there and listen to music. When I walked into his room, I fully expected my best friend to walk in behind me, as she often did. I knew nothing was wrong until I heard the click of his door lock.

I turned toward the door, which he was standing in front of and asked him why he had closed the door; he had never done that before. He mumbled something as he walked toward the stereo. A cold sensation raced down my spine. I no longer felt comfortable with the person I had called a friend for over six months. Deciding it was time to leave, I hastened to the door. I reached for it and began unlocking it when I felt him grab me. I never knew fear like I did at that moment. He yanked me away from the door and pushed me down. I fell into the table and chair that was against his wall. I felt a sharp pain, but that pain did not compare to his hand that grabbed me by my throat and tossed me onto the floor. My breath whooshed out of me when I hit the floor, hard. I lost my breath at the severe impact. Before I could blink, he was on top of me, grabbing at my clothes and forcing his leg between mine. I was not prepared for this violence, but I knew I had to protect myself at all costs. I began fighting for my life; I used every part of me to keep him from getting the thing he desired, my jewel. At 105 pounds I was no match for his 200 pounds, but I was going to fight until I had no more fight left. He took up the challenge. He began hitting me to stop my struggles, but I could not give up. Grabbing my arms with one hand, he held them above my head, cutting off my strikes. I was not completely defeated because I had legs, sturdy legs. I began moving around and using them to knee and kick him. He had been so busy trying to secure my arms he had moved off me a little. His movement gave me another tool to use to fight. I unleashed a hard knee close to his groin, and it was then I came face to face with the monster he had become; it was in his eyes that I saw the evil. The friend I had known was gone; in his place was a monster that was bent on robbing me of my voice and my power because of his selfish desire.

I continued to struggle. However, he was through dealing with my frantic movements. He stopped pulling at my belt and pants and used his free hand to grab the life out of me. Grabbing me by my throat again, he pushed against my windpipe. He let go of my arms so he could go back to his quest of removing my clothing. I used my freed hands to try to remove his hand from my throat, but I could barely breathe. I felt myself losing consciousness. He continued to apply pressure, and the darkness was coming for me. As it surrounded me, I closed my eyes and wondered if he would rape me while I was unconscious. Thoughts flowed through my mind. Would I live, or was this my last moment? Would my parents mourn me? What would my funeral be like; would many people attend? I could not think anymore I was falling, falling into the darkness when I heard a loud crash. My eyes popped open, and I saw my best friend rushing through the door and pulling my former friend off me. The stranger that was in the living room when we first came in tried to pull her away, but this 100-pound young woman found the strength to fight him off and move my would-be rapist. I could finally breathe again. Air filled my lungs, and I began coughing. My throat hurt, but it felt so good to draw breath. My friend pulled me off the floor and we rushed out of the apartment. We ran as fast as we could, terror overcoming both of us. All I could think of was his hand on my throat and I ran faster. We slowed down after running several blocks. We sat to catch our breath. Tears of fear, shame, betrayal, and joy mixed and streamed down my face. She tried to comfort me, but I would not let her close to me. As I calmed down, a car rolled slowly past us. It was him! He slowed, rolled his window down, and told me to get in the car. Without hesitation, my friend and I ran. We did not stop running until we made it back to campus.

I ran straight to my boyfriend's room. I did not care that the campus rule was that girls could not be in the boys' dorm rooms. No one tried to stop me, so I ran to his room and banged on his door. He opened the door after a few knocks, and I looked into the eyes of the man that loved me and I collapsed into his arms. After calming down, I told him about my experience. The arms that held and comforted me stiffened. The face that had looked at me with compassion and concern now looked at me with accusation. He pulled away and asked me a question that forever changed our relationship. "What did you do to cause him to do that to you?" My heart dropped and my soul froze. Did the man I trust just change on me? I looked into his face but instead of his face I saw the same evil I had seen in my almost rapist. He asked what I had been wearing when the assault happened, if what I had been wearing would have given our friend the wrong idea. I was offended, however, I stood and pointed to the baggy acid-washed jeans and the extra-large button-down plaid shirt I was wearing.

"This is what I was wearing," I said, spinning around. "How could this outfit give him wrong ideas?"

He had no response, just looked at me with a pained expression. He could not or would not meet my eyes. Instead, he suggested I lay down. I felt dirty, so I told him I would talk to him the next day and I went to my dorm and showered. I scrubbed and scrubbed, but I still felt the filth of my trauma. When the water turned to sharp icicles against my skin, I knew it was time to get out of the shower. I went into my room and turned to the only friend that understood me and could comfort me... the liquor bottle. We were under-aged, however, there were ways for a college student to get a bottle of alcohol. I took a long drink and relished in the burning sensation coating my bruised throat. The amber liquid took away some of the pain his heartless hand had caused me. As I continued to drink, the spirits coaxed me into a false sense of serenity, and I fell asleep. I woke up the next morning bleary-eyed and run-down. I did not know where I was or remember the events of the night before. My friends were in the room watching me with looks of concern on their faces. One was frowning, one was pacing back and forth, and my third friend, the hero of the evening before, sat on the bed next to me, kindness lighting her brown eyes. Looking at her brought it all back. Someone I trusted; someone I had called friend had nearly raped me. What had I done to cause it to happen? Question after question plagued my mind as tears began freely falling down my face. Again, my friend tried to comfort me and again I shrank back. I could not take the thought of anyone touching me, except for the man that had shut me out. My friends tried to advise me, but I would not hear it. They wanted me to go to the police and report it. I would not. They wanted me to tell our resident director, I would not. They soon tired of my stubbornness and left for class. I assured them I would be fine, and I would see them after class. As soon as the door closed, I got dressed and walked to the liquor store and bought myself some "forget my pain" in a bottle. Something that would not question me or try to get me to report something that I felt ashamed of. I walked back to my dorm room, and sat on my cold, narrow bed, took my shoes off, pulled the thick covers over me, and drank until I passed out.

This became my daily habit. For two weeks, I pretended to get ready for class, waited for my friends and roommate to leave, and grabbed a bottle of something alcoholic and consumed condemnation when I needed compassion. One morning the resident director summoned me; she wanted to see me right away. I just knew she had heard about all my drinking and since I was underaged, I feared she was going to kick me out. After showering, I put on some clean clothes and tried to sober up. She told me to sit down, and I grabbed a pillow and sat as far away from her as I could. I did not want her to get too close to me, she might have discovered my drinking. She began speaking in a soft tone, which was unlike her. She leaned in, moving a little closer, her eyes looked deeply into mine. Though her mannerisms were unusual, it was her words that jolted me. She knew. She knew I had almost been raped. I tuned her out and began trying to figure out how she knew. My heartbeat racing drowned out her words in my ears. My throat was warm, and I swallowed to retain my shame. When I couldn't control my erratic breathing any longer, I pulled my legs against my chest and began rocking. The walls were closing in like they did the night he touched me and went from friend to enemy. The night I was betrayed not only by him but also by my boyfriend. I had to get out of that room. I could no longer take thinking about that night. She told me that the police had been alerted and wanted to speak to me. They wanted me to press charges so he would not have the chance to hurt anyone else. I jumped up and told her no I would not press charges, I did not care if he got away with it and tried it again. There was no way I was going to tell the police anything. I would not repeat my secret. I did not wait to hear more. I ran from her room straight to a friend, a friend who would allow me to forget all of this, alcohol. I had to be careful though because people were around more. It was as if they knew I was on the brink of a breakdown and were there to pick up the pieces. I decided I had to learn how to function normally while drunk so people would not be suspicious. Instead of drinking throughout the day, I would drink late at night when everyone was asleep. Instead of drinking an entire bottle of liquor, I would only drink half of it. Pretending things were back to normal, I would hang out with my friends. I laughed, joked around, like I did before the incident, however on the inside I cried silent tears. I just wanted to be left alone with a pint. Everyone thought I was okay because I acted like I was; however, I was anything but okay.

As days turned into weeks, I noticed the looks I would get from others around campus. I watched the body language shift when I walked into a room. I had a new hurt, a new heartbreak. My boyfriend could not get over the incident and broke up with me. I could not handle the pain, so I picked up the bottle once again. I no longer cared about being a functional drunk I wanted my reality to change. How could I have gone from having a great relationship with a great guy to losing it all because someone wanted to violate me? I had no answers, but I was willing to do anything to change that night's events. I did something I had not done since I left Paterson, NJ almost a year before I picked up a bible. It was the bible my church had given me as a graduation gift. My aunt had always told me to read Psalms when I was in trouble, her scripture of choice was Psalm 122. She would tell me to read it over and over and get it into my spirit until I had peace. I had trouble and a lot of it, so I picked up the bible and went to that Psalm and read it over and over, maybe 13 times in all. My troubles did not change; my violation had not been erased and my boyfriend did not come back. I felt like I had wasted my time, I threw the bible down vowing never to pick it up again. That night I became a different person. I did not care about myself. I buried my emotions deep beneath sarcasm and pettiness. I kept people away, no one would get to see the real me anymore. I wore a mask and became someone that did not give a damn about anyone or anything. No one would hurt me again; this time I would do the hurting. Over the next 15 years I lived a life filled with rage, hurt, betrayal, and abuse. I suppressed that near fatal night. I never addressed it. And I carried on through those years with a huge chip on my shoulder and a hole in my heart where love should have been.

I had to learn how to release guilt and shame and learn that the events were not my fault, and I needed to forgive myself. No meant no, no matter what. I had to learn the truth. I was not to blame. In this situation, I was the victim, not the villain. I was innocent.

Andrea Joyce

The Storm: Heartbreak

"Even in laughter the heart may be in pain,
And the end of joy may be grief." Proverbs 14:13 (NASB)

"Heartbeat it makes me feel so weak". The song by Taana Gardner played in my head as I watched her mouth move, saying that my first real adult love, the father of my unborn child, my fiancé, had been cheating with her. She was the girlfriend of my boyfriend's best friend.

I dropped out of college after two years of poor decisions, destructive behavior, and bad class attendance. I returned to New Jersey, got a job, and started my life once again. I was living my life under my parents' roof, and it was hard returning to life before college. I had become accustomed to living on my own and making my own rules and decisions. You cannot do that living in someone else's house. I was also recovering from alcoholism that had plagued me for the last two years; I had been sober a few weeks before returning home. Since I wanted some of the freedom I had while attending college, my parents and I decided I needed my own place. I could only afford to stay at a boarding house, having just begun working. After packing up some of my things, I moved out and looked forward to my new life, making my own rules. That lasted a few hours. When my aunt and uncle heard I had moved out, they came, picked me up and moved me into their home. The rules at my aunt and uncles were more relaxed than at my parents' so it was a better fit for me. I worked hard, and I played hard. Partying from Thursday to Sunday in the clubs, dancing has always been my release. I worked at a sporting goods store six days a week, sometimes I worked a ten-hour shift. It was during one of these shifts that I met the then love of my life.

At the job I had amassed a group of friends that I hung out with after work. We would go to the clubs in New York and have a ball. We also went to the celebrity parties that happened around Englewood Cliffs in New Jersey. It became our custom to hang out every day after work, my partying was no longer limited to the Thursday-Saturday schedule. While at work one day, we began planning our night's mischief. While planning, long lines began forming because the store was pushing the new sneaker inventory it had gotten in. There was a huge sale, and everyone was taking advantage of it. I never paid attention to the customers. Customer service was not big on my radar at that time. I was a ring them up and get them out person. On this day, however, I looked out onto the floor and saw the finest man I had ever seen. He stood 6 foot 3 inches with a warm tan complexion highlighted by a golden white smile and sparkling green eyes. I was dumbstruck. He was wearing a bucket hat, t-shirt, Girbaud jeans and the latest pair of basketball sneakers. As I continued to stare at him, he looked up at me and currents went through my body. I never had such a potent attraction to anyone in my life, and I found it hard to breathe. The customer at my register tried unsuccessfully to get my attention. He cleared his throat, and I came out of my stupor. My two friends had also seen the eye candy before us and walked over to me. Both claimed him, but I knew in my heart that he was already mine. He continued to shop, and I would glance at him. Our eyes would connect and each time lightning bolts went through me. I did not know what the feeling was, but I knew I needed a distraction because I never acted that way. It wasn't like I had never seen an attractive guy before, but something about him shook me and it was obvious. I liked to play it cool, but he had me acting like a fan at a Michael Jackson concert. Eventually the lines receded. Although we had not spoken one word to each other, it felt like I knew him before, as if we had been together in another lifetime and were finally reconnecting. I turned my back to steady my heart and busy myself cleaning my station when lightning struck a direct hit.

"Excuse me," his deep musical voice said.

I knew, with everything within me, it was him. I felt him before I ever turned around. When I composed myself and remembered to breathe, I turned. His smile was infectious; we all returned his smile with big goofy ones of our own.

"I'm ready to check out," that melodious voice continued.

My girls raced to their registers and said they would help him. He was standing between their registers and mine. I sauntered over to my register and told him I could help him. Without hesitation, he walked over to my register and placed his item on the counter. I picked it up and our hands touched. I felt I was going to pass out right in that spot. The electricity that flowed between our hands could have restarted any dead heart, it revived mine. I promised myself that I would let no one get close to me after my near rape and breakup, but those promises flew out the window when I looked into his alarmingly green... wait were his eyes gold. Golden eyes? He had the prettiest golden green hazel eyes I had ever seen. Then he smiled at me and changed my life forever. I knew he was the one. He invited me out that same night after work and I agreed to not only go out with him but allowed him to pick me up from work that night. A rule I have only broken once, and only for him. That night began a whirlwind romance that would last for almost three years.

We hung out all the time. He introduced me to his family, and I introduced him to mine. I fell in love with his grandmother, who was raising him, and his sister who still lived with their father. His parents had divorced like mine and his father had remarried like mine; we had a lot in common. Most of my family members liked him, so we forged ahead with our relationship. We had good days and bad days like any couple, however, he always made me feel like the only person in his world. He lavished me with attention and gifts, and we went away on vacation several times. It wasn't long before he popped the big question and even though we were both young, I said yes. He wanted us to move to North Carolina and attend school together before we could go through with our plans, I found out I was pregnant. I was afraid of telling my family, so I began wearing baggy clothes again. When he found out that we were pregnant, he planned to transfer to a school in New Jersey and planned to be back within a few weeks. I was working full-time and taking classes at the local college. Either the heavy workload or the stress of the pregnancy was too much, because one evening I began bleeding heavily. I had been going to my regular doctor appointments and taking my prenatal vitamins, so I did not understand what was happening. I called one of my closest friends crying with fright. She came and took me to the emergency room. It seemed like an eternity passed before they called me to the back. By this time, the chair and I were covered in blood. I could not stand upright, so the orderlies rolled out a wheelchair and helped me in it. As I laid on the table while they doctor prodded and probed, I looked up to the colorless ceiling and prayed that my baby would be okay. The doctor's examination ended and with emotionless eyes, he stated that my baby girl had not made it. Ashley was gone; my first child, my first heartbeat had been taken and I could not bear it. I let out a horrific wail in that sterile, emotionless room. I cried and cried for a baby I would never know, I would never hold, I would never see grow up; I cried for the child created in love and taken before her time. My baby girl had died at the end of my second trimester. That stark, cold room became my child's last resting place, and I was inconsolable. They took the last of my baby and I left the hospital broken and shattered. Though losing my first child was the worst pain I could imagine, what happened next was even more devastating. I called my fiancé to tell him what happened. His sobs mixed with mine.

"Did you lose her on purpose? Did you kill my baby?" His pain and accusation mingled together, and the words hit my heart like hollow point bullets.

It struck me dumb; I could not believe that the man I loved with every fiber of my being had accused me of terminating my pregnancy or getting rid of our baby. Silence blanketed the phone while roaring thunder raged in my eardrums. His questions played on repeat in my mind, I can still hear its faint echo in my ears today. I hung up and crawled up the stairs in massive physical and new emotional pain. Feeling defeated I laid in bed wondering how one of the happiest times in my life could have turned into the second most horrible experience I had ever faced. Day turned into night turned into day and I did not notice, I was numb and wounded. I lost my baby girl and the trust of my fiancé. After not hearing from him for a week, I was shocked to see him walk into my aunt's house. Had he always been that fine? His hazel eyes were golden like the sun at golden hour. They held tears. I wanted to run into his arms and cry while he held me, but the last time I had done that my boyfriend had let me down. This time the person who I wanted to comfort me was the very one that hurt me. His questions had haunted me night and day. I would not go to him. We stood staring at each other unchecked tears in both of our eyes. We were two people that had lost a daughter and needed solace. He pulled me towards him and asked me to go on the porch with him. I fought tears and my emotions and followed him outside. It was during those moments that I could let go of the pent-up grief I had been holding onto. He more than anyone understood my sorrow because he felt it too. We talked, we cried, and we began healing.

After a few days we were back strong. We spent more time together than we did before he left for school. He was back to stay. If we weren't hanging in New Jersey, we were hanging at his place in New York. We talked about marriage again and decided we would marry in a year's time. I was floating on cloud 29. I was overjoyed with the thought of being his wife and having his children. Funny how the best laid plans fall apart the closer you get to them. We decided to tell our family about our engagement, but first he wanted to go away and celebrate with his best friend and his best friend's girl. He wanted to do a couple's trip. I took time off work, so that we could enjoy a week at the beach. Since my fiancé was paying for everything, his friend volunteered to drive us to the airport. They picked me up first. We were filled with excitement, singing and dancing to the songs on the radio, planning what we were going to do at the beach. Pulling up to his best friend's girl's house we all got out of the car and danced around. I did not know what was in store for me.

He pulled me in for an embrace and then turned me around and wrapped his arms around me. The back of my head was lying on his chest as we swayed to a love song playing. I couldn't help but think how I was going to enjoy our life together. Picturing our home, and our future, a shrill voice screaming pulled me from my reverie.

"Who is that bitch? Who is she?"

I turned in his arms to look at a pretty brown-skinned girl walking down the stairs. I mean she would have been pretty if her face were not contorted into an angry scowl. Her nose flared, her eyes bulged, and her face was red. I saw beads of sweat rolling down her face. I was confused. Why was this girl yelling and more importantly who was she calling a bitch?

I asked him what was going on, but before he could answer his best friend walked up to her and asked what her problem was. She shocked us all with her response.

"Why did he bring that bitch here to my house?"

I had the answer to one question. I now knew who she was talking about, me. As I began taking off my chains and my earrings, he pulled me in tighter. He whispered for me to calm down and ignore her, then he kissed me. Now, I was upset. I did not tolerate disrespect; however, his kisses were made of magic; they always had the power to erase my thoughts. I calmed down, but she continued.

"Oh, so now you're going to kiss the bitch?"

That was one bitch too many. I pulled away from his arms and walked over to her. I wanted to know what her issue was so I could fix the problem for her. He was behind me, and his best friend was beside her, telling her to stop being rude. His friend asked her what her problem was for the third time, and she shed light on her issue.

"He and I are messing around. He was supposed to dump you and it was supposed to be just me and him going away this weekend."

The world stopped turning and the roar of thunderclaps was back in my ears. I felt myself getting hot, and faint. What had she just said? Surely, she did not just tell me the man I was engaged to, the father of the child I had just miscarried, was cheating on me. There was no way he could cheat; we were always together. Then I thought about the time he was late picking me up, smelling as fresh as a daisy when he was supposed to have been working out in the scorching sun all day. He had been freshly showered. I thought about the time he was supposed to go the fair with me and a group of my friends, but something came up. I thought about his distraction the last few weeks and it all made sense. For as good as he treated me, sometimes he was inattentive and missing in action. I turned to look at him and his eyes told me the story. Those beautiful golden green eyes I had loved for almost three years told me of his betrayal. He lowered them, refusing to meet my questioning eyes any longer. I hit him with the force of all the pain I felt from the disloyalty and the pain I endured when he questioned me about losing our baby. That 6-foot 3-inch giant fell back, and I saw nothing but a red curtain. I could see nothing, but my blind fury and I unleashed hit after hit until I felt myself flying in the air and being held. When I came to myself his best friend was holding me and my fiancé was on the ground.

The treachery was not just in him cheating on me, but the person with whom he cheated. His best friend's girl. Their disloyalty to both of us set me off again and this time I went for her. The person who had been so outspoken and arrogant and who had called me a female dog, suddenly backpedaled. She was apologizing and begging for forgiveness. I wanted them to both hurt the way they had hurt me. I wanted to repay them right there and then for the pain their lust and selfishness caused, but it was his best friend who calmed the situation. He too had been affected by their deception. With tears pouring down his face he asked the million-dollar question.

"Why?"

It was then that the reality of their duplicity hit everyone. All that could be heard from the four of us was weeping and whimpers. Their infidelity would forever change our lives; there was no going back to the way it used to be. Friendships would be broken, and relationships severed. He reached out to me, but I was too wounded. I could not give him the solace he sought. He had taken me back to the very moment of my last trauma and this time there would be no coming back. His friend got in his car and told me to get in. Some small part wanted me to kiss him in front of them so they could feel what I felt, but the bigger part of me could never hurt him like that. I got in the car with him begging me to stay, begging me for another chance, but I could not. I could no longer feel anything because my heart had frozen and shattered. Reaching through the window I dropped my engagement ring on the ground as we pulled off. I can still hear his cries.

He tried many times and many ways to reconcile, however I had grown up with the philosophy "give no one a second chance". Forgiveness was nothing I knew about then. I just could not give him a second chance; it went against everything I was taught. As was my routine, I did not deal with that heartbreak. Instead, I got into relationship after relationship trying to forget my love for him, giving no one all of me. How could I when my heart had frozen? I pretended to be happy, but my heart pined for him.

I tried to forget him by rushing into another relationship. That relationship produced my daughter. My family suggested that I marry him to give my child a last name. I did not want to marry him because I was still in love with my ex-fiancé but since I did not want my child to feel like an outcast, I married her father. During the ceremony as I repeated my vows, I had my fingers crossed and said it was not real. I knew I did not love him, but I wanted to make my family happy. The day after we said "I do" he left to go on a military tour of duty for a year. He was assigned overseas. Two or three weeks later we separated. Once we separated, I was ready to get back into the dating scene. I was trying to get over my ex by getting with the next, I felt no loyalty to my then husband because he was the rebound that went wrong. I had a lot of pain stored up, not just the heartbreak that my ex-fiancé caused me, but the pain I caused him.

Right after my nuptials, he showed up to my parents' house. It was not the first time he had shown up. He had come to my dance rehearsals, my aunt and uncle's house, my job, but this time was different. He came bearing gifts for me and my daughter and he came bearing his heart. My mother reluctantly let him in, he carried an enormous bouquet in his hand and an enormous teddy bear under his arm. I stared at him in confusion. Why was he there, and more importantly had he always been that fine? As I stood there with my mouth open and my eyes unblinking, he got down on his knee and begged for my forgiveness. He then said that he wanted to marry me and be a father to my daughter who should have been his in the first place. My heart stopped. Why had I not given him a second chance before I married someone else? Everything I wanted was kneeling in front of me with flowers, a teddy bear for my daughter, and an opened ring box in his hands. But I could not marry him because I was already married. With tears flowing down my face, I looked at him and said the words I didn't want to say to him.

"I can't."

I told him I could not marry him. He begged for another chance, and I wanted to give it to him but instead I told him I was already married. He let out a wail that dropped me to my knees. I grabbed him into a hug and our pain mingled. We cried for a long time until he broke our embrace. He stood up, threw down the flowers and bear and walked out of the door and my life without looking back. That pain hurt as much as his infidelity and betrayal had. I began resenting my husband and my family for talking me into getting married. The "if only's" began. If only I had forgiven him, if only I had given him a second chance, if only I had never messed around with my husband, if only I had not married him, if only I had stood my ground and told my family no, and on and on. I carried that heartache for decades and made unhealthy relationship decisions because of it. I grieved the two greatest losses of my life, Ashley, and him.

I needed to learn how to heal.

The Storm: Betrayal

"Even my close friend,
    someone I trusted,
one who shared my bread,
    has turned[a] against me." Psalms 41:9 (NIV)

Best Friends Forever, so I thought.

I have had friendships I thought would last a lifetime, however I was proven wrong. I remember growing up and my aunt would tease me about some of my friends. She would say you bend over backwards for them, but can you say they do the same for you. Of course, I defended them because surely people would treat me the way I treated them. We lived by a code, the friend code. As friends it was an unspoken rule that you did not talk to, date, sleep with, nor marry, the significant other or the ex-significant other of your friend.

There was a friend I had since high school I hung with strong. Wherever you saw me, you saw her and vice versa. I felt bad because she was an only child, so I invited her everywhere I got invited to. My family said she was jealous of me, but it was hard to comprehend someone I cared about being jealous of me. Jealous why? She was pretty and popular; she had celebrities wanting to date her. Her hair was always laid, and her outfits were always flawless. I laughed at my family. They said keep your friends away from your man, I chuckled. She had a man, and I trusted her. I had three close friends however they did not like each other. I would spend time with them separately. Each one said the other two were not real friends and to watch my back. It was funny because they were correct about each other; none of the three could be trusted.

One day while eating dinner at my aunt's house I received a call. The call was from a blast from the past, the ex-boyfriend of my best friend. He wanted to wish me well. He had heard about the birth of my child and subsequent marriage. I thanked him and asked about his family and his life. I teased him about his real reason for calling, he was fishing for information about my friend and that was when the truth was revealed.

"Are you two still friends after what she did?" he asked.

"Of course, we are still friends and she has done nothing to me," I said as my stomach began fluttering.

His laugh was without humor. "She and your ex messed around while you were dating him."

It was my turn to laugh without humor. "You have the story mixed up. He messed around with her cousin while I was away at college. I know all about it."

"That's half the story," he responded, "she started sleeping with him before she introduced him to her cousin. It's the reason she and I broke up."

I didn't believe him; this was my best friend for over nine years. She would not betray me. He proved it to me and used three-way calling to do it. He first called my ex to corroborate the story. My ex did not know I was on the phone; I was muted. They had been best friends for years, but their friendship had been cut off. I never knew why.

After announcing himself my best friend's ex got straight to the point of his call.

"Did you sleep with Andrea's friend?"

"Man, we already talked about this. Why are you bringing it back up after all this time?"

"Answer the question," her ex replied.

"Yes, we messed around for a while," my ex stated.

"While you were with Andrea?"

"You already know what happened," he said.

"Don't make me whoop off on you again," her ex growled.

"Why are you bothering me with this now? We already talked about it. Yes, I slept with her while I was with Andrea," my ex said slamming down the phone.

My friend's ex said nothing. In the silence I found myself at a loss. I was unsure of how to feel. It had taken place several years before but since I just found out about it, it felt like the betrayal had happened right at that moment. I wanted to lay hands on her, and I do not mean in the biblical way. Why was I so angry about something that had happened years before? This was my trusted friend; I had done a lot for her and even included her in my family and friendships. I defended her when others talked about her. I was a genuine friend to her, and I expected the same in return. Not only had she hooked him up with her cousin, but she had also been sleeping with him too. There was no coming back from this betrayal. I was beyond irrational with rage. Before I could utter a word, he dialed another number.

"Hello," my best friend said.

"I just talked to your boy," he taunted.

"Do not call me with your foolishness. I told you I was sorry. It happened over five years ago. Why are you still bringing it up?" she asked.

"Because I can't believe you betrayed me and your best friend. How could you do that to both of us?"

"How many times do we have to go over this? Yes, I slept with him and yes it was while he was with her. Yes, I introduced him to my cousin after. I am sorry that it happened, but it's over. I will not keep talking about it. Don't call me with this stupid stuff anymore," she said before hanging up.

I thanked him for the information and hung up. I could not believe that she and my ex had been sleeping together. She had the audacity to answer the questions without remorse. Her voice held sarcasm and contempt, not for him but for me. My aunt's and mother's warnings came back to me. I had let a snake into my life, and it had bitten me. Unfortunately, she was not the only snake I have had to endure.

One day I must thank the phone company because had it not been for three-way calling, I would have been forever in the dark.

One of the other friends in my best friend circle also thought it was their right to betray our friendship. She did me a huge favor or at least that was her reasoning for me to not end our friendship. I had been telling her about a man I dated I had known since I was a pre-teen. We had run into each other a few months after my separation and began talking, it got serious. He wanted to be exclusive, and he wanted me to file for divorce, so he could marry me. I drug my feet because I was still nursing that broken heart but gave in and we became exclusive. He planned out this huge future for us. While I liked him, I know my feelings did not mirror his. What made us work was that he did not live in the state I lived in, so we did not see each other often. He would come up twice a month and I used my child as the reason I could not go see him. His calls and visits took my mind off my heart ache, and I appreciated that. I did not want to keep pining for my ex-fiancé, so he was my distraction.

Out of the blue, one balmy Sunday afternoon, another best friend in my circle called me and asked me about him. I told her he had been there the weekend before with an engagement ring. I told her I turned him down because I was still married and was not looking to get remarried anytime soon. She was interested in the details of his visit and asked me to call him on three way so she could say hi. This was not the first time they had spoken. She was with me when I ran into him again and he had even tried to hook her up with a friend of his. We had often talked on the phone together, so her request was normal. I dialed his number, and he answered. When he heard my voice, his southern accent became even more animated.

"Hey baby," he said, "I've been thinking about next weekend. Let's rent a hotel at the shore. This way your daughter can get to know me. It's time for us to meet so she will be comfortable with me being in your life and we can work on getting married. You know how much I love you, let's be a family."

Before I could tell him that my friend was on the phone too, she interrupted.

"Love her, marry her? Are you for real? How are you going to marry her when you love me," she raged, "you were supposed to tell her about us, how we have been sleeping together for two months. Tell her you sent for me and my daughter and we stayed with you for a weekend the first time and a week the second time. Tell her that my daughter calls you daddy, and you told me we would be a family.

I sat stunned as I heard about their affair from her mouth. She shared their intimate details and her belief that he was going to drop me for her. He remained silent until her tirade ended. I sat wide eyed with my mouth open. Was this another person I trusted in my inner circle that had slept with someone I was dating? And this time it was not an ex, this was a current relationship. Before I could respond, he spoke.

"Baby please," he said the sound of tears in his voice.

Which baby was he talking about, the one he was in a relationship with or the one he was cheating with?

"I'm sorry," he continued, "please forgive me."

I had one question and one question only.

"How did you two contact each other? I never gave you her number, and I never gave you his number," I asked.

He confessed; she approached him and flirted with him, and he flirted back. They moved on from flirting to exchanging body fluids over the last few months. I was not upset with him; I was just dating him and even though we were in a relationship I had never been intimate with him. It was easy for me to cut him out of my life because my heart was still with another. My friend was a different story. I was beyond hurt I trusted her and allowed her in my world. I had helped her out of some situations and was there when her family turned their backs on her. The only thing I expected in return, was loyalty. Silly me, I thought she understood that. Anyone I was dating was off limits. Instead of having an altercation, I bowed out of the friendship.

The third friend in my circle of best friends did not sleep with a man of mine. She stopped talking to me because I had to tell her no. She was angry because she thought I could help her out of a situation and because I had to tell her no, she began saying nasty things about me and even had another supposed friend contact me with threats. It was heart breaking because I valued my friendship with her. To have it end because of the word no was ridiculous. Some of my friends were friends just to get things from me. As soon as they could no longer get anything from me, they turned their friendship off.

There have been many people who held the title "best" friend with me, and they showed themselves to be the worst friends. I realized I was more of a friend to them than they were a friend to me. If they needed me, I was there. I brought them into my life and heart. I was the one who called, who visited and who invited them out. Days would go by, if I did not call them, they would not call me. I would bend and contact them, and they would act as if not being in touch for weeks was normal. When I needed an ear to listen or a shoulder to cry on, I could rarely get it, so I changed how I was a friend. I matched their energy. If they did not call, I did not call. I broke off conversations that were one-sided. If they made me listen to their issues, but they got busy or preoccupied when I began speaking, the next time they called I would find a reason to get off the phone. I became unavailable. I stopped answering calls and turned down invitations. As I met new people, I gave them the title of friend but deep down I already knew that I would not let them get too close to me. I tried to give no one the opportunity to be in my heart anymore.

I had to learn that not everyone who shouted friend was a friend.

The Storm: Homelessness

"Jesus replied to him, 'Foxes have holes and the birds of the air have nests, but the [a]Son of Man has nowhere to lay His head.'" Matthew 8:20 (NKJV)

You can never go home again.

I heard people say that once they left their hometown for a few years and went back, it was never the same. While living in Atlanta, I found myself in another complicated relationship that I wanted to evolve into marriage. After seven years, I realized it was not, so I moved on. I was still carrying despair from my broken engagement, disappointment from my first marriage, disloyalty from my next relationship, deception on my part in my next love connection, and now disillusionment. There was never a moment between ages 17-33 that I was not involved with someone. I carried all the baggage I picked up from one relationship and brought it into my new relationship, never unpacking, and it became heavier and heavier.

After ending my seven-year relationship, I decided I was tired of dating and wanted to be married. I said whoever the next man was that I dated I would marry because I did not want to meet anyone else. I did not want to love anyone else I just wanted to settle down and be done with all the dating and relationship drama. Be careful what you ask for because it might just pop up. The next person I met, I indeed married. It was not a good fit. I married someone I was not compatible with; someone I had no connection to or chemistry with and even worse someone again that I did not love. It was a pattern. Without love, God, respect and fidelity, the marriage quickly crumbled. One thing about marriage, when you say "I Do" you pick up each other's good and bad situations. Everything affects you if you are the responsible party or not. If they are in debt, you are in debt. If they do not pay a bill, it counts against you too. I watched as things began piling up, I wanted to be the "good wife" and allow my husband to lead, however he was leading us into the poor house. My good credit score moved to a piss poor credit rating, my savings eaten up, and we were evicted from one place after another.

A series of events happened that would forever change my life. Although I just welcomed a son, I was tired of my marriage. I found out that my stepdad was diagnosed with stage 4 cancer, and I discovered I was pregnant, again. Because of fidelity issues I had stopped sleeping with my husband a couple of months before, so I did not understand how I could be pregnant, I was shocked. It is true, it only takes one time. I was ready to leave my marriage, but I could not see how I could make it with 2 children and one on the way. I felt trapped. During this time, my dad, the man who raised me after saying "I Do" to my mom, passed away. Although I knew stage 4 was the last stage, I believed a miracle would happen and my dad would be brought back to full health. Well, he was, just not here. I remembered one of the last conversations he and I had. In the hospital room, my dad looked in my eyes and said, "if a man cannot treat you as well as I do, you don't need to be with him. All your life I treated you like a princess and that is what you deserve." I had never told my dad or mom what I had gone through in my marriage, so for him to say that I knew I needed to make some changes in my life. When he was put on life support even though he was not conscious, I knew he heard me when I told him I was going to name my youngest daughter after him and that I would honor his words. I thought back over the years of our relationship and how he went from being my mother's boyfriend to my mother's husband. I thought about the plans I made to break them up and then accepting him as my dad. He was never my stepfather because he treated me as his flesh and blood. This man chose to love me despite all the hell I put him through, I was just sad that I missed out on years of embracing it. After the funeral, I went into a deep depression, a valley of sorrow. If something did not change and quick, I felt I would explode. Well things changed. The husband that did not want to work enlisted in the military and went away to basic training. We separated. I needed to be surrounded by family, friends, and familiarity.

I packed up my bags and drove home to Paterson, New Jersey. I moved back into my parents' home, but it seemed unreal. My dad was no longer there, and I now had three children to care for. It was difficult being back in my parents' home as an adult child with children and after a year, I moved out. My temporary work assignment ended a few weeks after moving in and I struggled to find another position. After a few months of fruitless searches, the landlord came and did the very thing I feared. The kids and I were asked to vacate the premises, and he put a padlock on the door. I did not know what to do. When I had gone through eviction before I had a Plan B and sometimes a Plan C. This time I had nothing. I could not go back to my mother and ask her to move back in and I did not want to ask my friends for help. I felt like I had no options, so that night the kids and I stayed in the van outside of our apartment and slept.

In the morning I woke with no plan, but I knew I had to get the children to school. We drove to a fast-food restaurant and went into the women's bathroom. We bathed and brushed our teeth in the sink and the kids wore the same uniform they had been wearing the day before. After dropping them off to school I took a few of the dollars to buy them some clothes and also bought blankets and pillows since it was winter in New Jersey and the nights were freezing. While the kids were at school, I went to the library and applied for jobs. I had a pre-paid cell phone that only took a few dollars to keep on. I applied for unemployment because I figured any money coming in would be a help. They told me it would take from a few weeks to a few months for them to process my claim. I also went down to social services to request housing, food, and medical help. Since I had no permanent address and since I had no way of guaranteeing money for rent the next month, they turned me down. Frustration began rising in me; however, I did not want to add any additional pressure to the kids. I just dealt with my oldest daughter's tears because her classmates had teased her about her book bag having a foul smell. She had been carrying around a snack of cookies and milk. The milk opened and spilled into her bag and got over all her bag and papers in the bag. We had been living in the van for a few weeks. I was down to the last few dollars and did not know what else to do. I applied for everything that I could, but it was one closed door after another. Taking the last of the money I went to the store and bought her a new book bag.

By now we had a set routine. The kids and I would wake in the morning and go to one of two fast-food places to wash up, the employees were used to our faces and treated us nicely. I would drop them off to school where they were guaranteed to get breakfast, lunch, and a snack. I would go to the library to look for jobs until my time was over; you were only allowed on the computers for a certain length of time. Then I would go to the park and make phone calls until it was time to pick the kids up from school. I would take them to the library or the bookstore so they could do their homework. I am so grateful to one bookstore in particular; it was a haven for me and the kids for many days of our homelessness. The kids would sit at the tables and do their work and then read books or take part in an activity the bookstore was having. We would stay there in its warmth until they closed for the night. I was sad to see those bookstores shut down a few years later. Sometimes I would take them to the park so they could play for a little while and not have to be cooped up in the van. I would go to a fast-food place and sometimes be able to buy them a children's meal, sometimes all I could afford was one hamburger that we would split. This was our day from start to finish for months. And I was not sitting on my laurels, I harassed temporary agencies, employment agencies, and anyone I could for a job. Doors and opportunities continued to close. After a couple of months, I had no money, about a quarter tank of gas and no ideas. I received an unexpected phone call. One of my church members and friends called requesting a ride the next day. I wanted to say no when she said three magical words.

"I'll pay you."

Those rides became a blessing for a few weeks, she would ask for rides and sometimes give me $5 for gas, sometimes $20. What she did not realize was that money would go towards not only gas, but food and visits to the laundromat. The kids only had three sets of clothes, the uniforms they were wearing when we were evicted and the two pairs of jeans and t-shirts I bought from the store, so it was imperative that I go to the laundromat at least once a week. She did not know about our situation, but her kindness allowed us to continue to live with dignity. No one knew we were homeless for almost four months. I kept it to myself never asking for help.

I had to learn how to let go of pride and ask for help.

The Storm: Addiction

"Woe to those who rise early in the morning so that they may pursue intoxicating drink,

Who stay up late in the evening so that wine may inflame them!"
Isaiah 5:11 (NASB)

Andrea Joyce

Nothing tastes as sweet...

While we were homeless and I was trying to find work, I fell into a dangerous habit. I began eating mint. Not just any kind of mint, the soft cubed ones that dissolved upon contact. Now before you laugh and say how was this an addiction, let me continue. Remember I told you that the kids would have two guaranteed meals while in school and something else to eat at night. I would be at the library, park, bookstore or somewhere trying to find a job. I did not have money to eat. If I had eaten breakfast or lunch, it would have thrown our money off. So instead of breakfast and lunch I began eating the dissolving peppermint. At first it was two or three of the candies at a time. Then it became five or six and that number jumped to ten. I would eat them in rapid succession trying to curb the hunger I was feeling. Because it was the only substance I was getting, my body craved it as often as possible. I graduated from buying a tub of the mint a week, to buying a tub every three-four days and when they were on sale, I was over the moon.

I did not even see it as an addiction, I thought I was just popping candy to help me get over my hunger. The kids were concerned because they never saw me eat anything else. Even when we had enough money to each get a meal, I would pass and just eat mints. As time moved on my mint intake increased to buying the tubs every other day to eventually finishing a tub in a single day.

I thought it was something that would end once we got into a stable situation. A friend discovered our homelessness and moved us into her home. Soon after my mother learned of our plight and secured housing for us. We were fortunate to move into a house and they approved me for unemployment. I thought with all the good that was happening, I would walk away from my mint habit. After I purchased a tub of mint, I promised myself that would be it. I would not waste my money buying anymore. As I neared the last few mints, I felt strong and determined. I was eating regular meals. I was eating at least twice a day, and I felt better. When the tub was gone, I threw it away with great pride and did not think about mint again, for a day. The next day I went looking for mint in the van, in my purse, and in my pockets. I felt like I just needed one more to hold me over and I would be done forever. Not so. When I could not find one more mint, I went to the store and bought a bag. I finished that bag in a matter of minutes and I walked back into the store and bought a tub. I told myself I would not eat all the candy, I just wanted to have it around for emergencies. After all everyone wanted fresh breath. A day later I went back to the store to replace the empty mint container I had in my van. I was hooked, but I kept telling myself I was not addicted to the candy, the sugar. I tried many times to stop, even once doing an abrupt withdrawal. It was not by choice. I had gone to my usual store to buy the mint, and they did not have the tub or the bag. No problem, I would get it from somewhere else. That day I went to 5 stores, and no one had my mint, and I must be honest, I went a little stir crazy. I was craving the mint; it was like I could taste it. I looked for the candy every day for five days. Never once did I say forget it and walk away. I just looked for it more and more until that sixth day when the store had restocked it. I was overjoyed and for the next two years I gave in to my addiction every day. I did not see any issues with my addiction; it would not be for another two-three years until the impact of all that sugar would take a toll on me physically.

When I moved back to Atlanta, I thought everything would be smooth. I obeyed God and moved back to where He called me to be. I ran to New Jersey to hide out and lick my wounds, like Moses had run away to Midian after killing the Egyptian slave-master. But like Moses, I had to return to the place that God called me to be because I had work to do. I was blessed to live with my sister for a few months then find my own place. I had a job and met a couple that opened their arms to me and invited me to write on their web series. It was the beginning of my training to own a production company. I thought I was flying high and then the effects of all that sugar came back to haunt me. It started out discretely. I was eating, and I chipped a tooth on the side. While I did not like the appearance it gave me, it was nothing I was too concerned about. A few months later I chipped another tooth and again I did not dwell on it because it was not in the front. Then the unthinkable happened, while eating ice I broke my front teeth, they cracked and split. It would be the beginning of me not being able to hide the loss of my teeth. I was not a vain person, but your teeth are your glory, everyone looks in your mouth when you talk and when you smile. I was in a field where I was in the limelight. How could I move forward with the shame of having no top teeth? I did not move forward in the limelight. I hid out on the couch of my apartment and cried for a year. How could I speak the Word of God, how could I produce shows without teeth? A friend suggested I go to the dentist so they could offer solutions to my issue. I went with high hopes, I was sure there were others who had to have a cosmetic repair on their teeth. My dreams were dashed when they told me they could help me, but the cost was astronomical. I had no job, no insurance and was barely keeping up with rent how was I going to afford thousands of dollars to fix my teeth?

I decided I would be a hermit the rest of my life. I was already hosting an inspirational talk show online, no one could see me. I began working for an online customer service company, so there was no real reason for me to go outdoors. My seclusion was not to be as God pushed me into ministry at my church. I was called to teach and speak to the masses. At first, when I spoke, I would talk and laugh behind my hand. That drew more attention to my mouth. I tried to change the way I spoke closing my lips around my mouth more, so people could not see the inside of my mouth and I began lowering my head when I talked. I did not want to see reactions to my oral condition. I stopped looking people in the face to avoid the looks of horror and disgust. I avoided all eyes. My teeth became my shame. And they still are since they remain unfixed. My mindset is just a little different. I don't hide in seclusion anymore; however, I hide in plain sight. When I speak to audiences, I do not look at anyone, I look at a wall or door behind them. I fear meeting new people because I will see that look in their eyes and hear the question in their mind, "yuck, what happened to her teeth?" Dating has become a nightmare; you cannot hide your mouth when you are sitting across from someone eating and talking. I expect men to be turned off by me, so I don't put forth an effort anymore. I settled for anyone because I did not feel like a man of quality would select me. I have lost job opportunities because of this thorn in my side. While it might not have been my teeth that caused me to lose out, my demeanor did. It is so hard to look at someone in the eyes and see the condemnation in theirs. It even caused me to give up on one of my dreams. I am a dramatic person; acting was in my genes since birth. However, when I lost my teeth, I decided to work behind the camera instead of in front of it. Writing, directing, and producing became the loves of my life because the thought of being on camera frightened me. Actors I was in a scene with would see my mouth and would be grossed out by my appearance. Even when humor fills my soul, my hand rushes to my shame reminding me of my addiction. My addiction became my crutch and now it is my cross to bear. Its negative effects enduring far past my last mint.

I had to learn to stop relying on crutches.

Andrea Joyce

The Storm: Suicide

"Do not be excessively wicked, and do not be foolish. Why should you die [a]before your time?" Ecclesiastes 7:17 (NASB)

I looked at my reflection and the mirror revealed the monster that was lurking inside.

After moving into the house and receiving unemployment, I thought my life would settle down. We were good for a few weeks and then a tremendous, unexpected, and severe hurricane stormed through my life, and I had no life jacket or boat.

The superstorm raged when I walked outside to take the kids to school and discovered my van was gone. In New Jersey we have alternate side parking for street cleaning. I parked on the right side of the street, so my van could not have been towed. My next thought was that it was stolen. I was confused because I had an alarm on the car and if someone broke into it, I would have heard it. Then I looked around for broken glass because how would a thief have been able to steal the car without getting inside of it. There was no broken glass. After a few minutes of standing on the street in confusion, my neighbor came out and told me a repo company towed my car. I am still not sure how she knew that but was grateful for the information. I placed a call to the dealership where we purchased the vehicle and was told that they had been trying to contact my husband for payment without success for three months. Since the vehicle was in his name, they had not contacted me. It amused me that every other bill I got contacted whether or not I was on the account, but the vehicle I had possession of, the place where my children and I lived for months was not in my name and they did not communicate with me. I tried not to give into my frustration and called my estranged husband. He advised he would no longer be paying for anything since divorce papers were filed. After a few choice words I disconnected the call. I had to plan a way to get the kids back and forth to school. Once that puzzle was solved, I thought I had seen the worst of the storm.

The feeder bands of my life's hurricane came in the form of another betrayal. While out with some friends I ran into a childhood friend.

Many thought that we had been in a relationship in the past, but the truth was we were platonic friends. This time however, we could not deny the attraction between us. We exchanged numbers and went out. One date turned into two and so on. We became serious and spent a lot of time together. We clicked well, and I began falling in love. My commitment to church was paramount having re-established my relationship with God. I was active in several ministries, including liturgical dance and ministers in training class. I wanted to do right by God, however the temptations were too powerful to turn down. I struggled in my quest to do right and be right and I was losing. After speaking to my spiritual father, I backed out of ministry for a while feeling I could not give up the connection I had with this man. I thought we would be together forever. I had finally broken the cycle of poor relationships and found the one I was supposed to be with. The unexpected heavy rains and gusty winds of the feeder bands hit full force. A friend and I were out hanging with my forever love, when he announced he had something to tell me. He told me he had been keeping a secret but wanted to clear the air. He grabbed my hands, looked into my eyes, and told me that he was engaged to be married and would be getting married within the month. He explained that he was conflicted because he loved and wanted to be with me, however he felt obligated to marry his fiancée because she stuck by him through a tough period in his life. Even though he did not love her, the duty he felt toward her was strong. His lips kept moving, however I heard no sound because the world as I knew it stopped. I was transported back to the sidewalk, standing beside my fiancé watching his best friend's girl's lips move. Was this what my fiancé had done? Had he wined and dined his best friend's girl and plied her with promises and romantic expressions? Had he led her on, like I had been led on? What did he mean engaged? I had given up ministry for this man, and even though my divorce papers were filed I was not divorced, so I was breaking a commandment for this man, no wait I was breaking two because he and I were not married. I wanted to scream, cry, and fight, but I was numb. I lived and breathed this man; he was only the second man to have pricked my heart since the breakup of my engagement. The void that I thought his love filled left a larger emptiness than ever before and I was helpless.

The storm raged as I became colder inside. Unfortunately, I was also cold outside. I realized that instead of having to pay just for the gas and electric, in an older home, I had to pay for coal to heat it. I could barely keep up with the rent, gas, and electric this was another cost. We moved in when it was warm, and I was unaware of how expensive coal was. Its expense was more than the gas and electric combined. New Jersey is a state that begins getting cold in September, so if we wanted to be warm, we were going to need a lot of coal. In the beginning my mother helped pay for it, but it became too much for her; she had her own bills. I paid for coal when I could, but after a while I could no longer afford it. The kids and I began staying in the front room so we could use a heater to warm us. We slept in clothes and coats to keep warm. It was not uncommon to wake up and see our breath in the room as we spoke.

'Twas the night before Christmas when the eye of the storm hit. I was driving my mother's car to the hardware store and was parking when a strange sensation came over me. It felt a little like dizziness, a little like vertigo. I was seated, and the spell passed shortly. A neighboring car misjudged the parking space and sideswiped my mother's car. I went into a panic and was relieved to see that the damage was a barely noticeable dent. The driver offered to pay to get the dent fixed and provided their insurance and contact information. I knew it would upset my mother but my concern was returning her car so I could lie down. Once I parked her car, I drove mine over to a friend's house to pick up the kids who were celebrating an early Christmas since I would not be coming out of the house the next day. My mom had gone South to take care of business, and I was staying at her house so the kids and I could have heat for a while. While waiting for the kids to get ready, I began rubbing my left eye because it felt strange. I ignored it because I was eager to get home for the day. Christmas morning the kids opened their gifts, and we were fixing breakfast. As we sat down, I picked up my juice glass and began drinking, well, dribbling was more like it. I could not wrap my lips over the glass rim. I did not understand what was happening. I walked into the bathroom and had the shock of my life. The left side of my face was drooped downward. I also could not communicate clearly. I sounded like the character from that Saturday morning cartoon where the young man sounded like he had a mouthful of mush. Thinking I had a stroke I became paralyzed with fear. I did not want to say anything to the kids because I did not want to worry them, but it terrified me. I prayed maybe I had a reaction to the accident and when I woke up in the morning, my face would be normal. No such luck, my face was worse the next day. I feared going to the hospital because I did not want to hear that I had, had a stroke or worse. I did the only thing I could, I hid out from everyone.

No one knew I had an issue with my face because I stopped going to church, I ducked my Pastor's calls and I stayed away from my friends. No one in my family, besides my children, knew I had an issue. The storm surge hit hard. I was alienated from my family. After learning of the damage to her car, my mother and I stopped speaking. It upset her that I used her car without permission, especially since she had given me a van to use. A family member called me and threatened to call social services on me and have my kids taken away. We were back to staying in the icehouse and every day I watched my kids trying to stay warm. Unemployment was running out and food was low. The kids were growing out of their clothes, school tuition was unpaid, and I was getting constant calls about making the balances current. A friend persuaded me to go to the hospital. She rode with me to make sure I went, and we met another friend there. The doctor advised me I had Bell's palsy, a condition that crippled your face. He told me if I did not take the prescribed steroids my face might take up to a year to heal on its own, if at all. The doctor also explained I could not suddenly stop taking the steroid because it could kill me.

He prescribed the medications, and it felt as if the walls were closing in on me and I had no way of escape. It was one bad thing after another, and it became too much.

After dropping the kids off to school, instead of going to the library, park, or bookstore like usual, I went back to the house. There was a heaviness on me I could no longer take. I had been wearing wigs that hid my face. I walked into the bathroom and snatched off my disguise and looked into the mirror at the monster who looked back. I saw all the heart ache etched on my chocolate skin, heard the taunts of the kids calling me blackie and midnight deafening all reason, saw the father who neglected me and the boy that rejected me, and saw the failed relationships and the broken friendships. Homelessness and addiction played on my mirror's movie dragging me far into despair. Violation and alienation, a little girl longing for her parents to love her and validate her. Her eyes longing for her family to make her feel included. I saw the teenager who like the black sheep instead of embracing her differences and seeing her beauty turned to rebellion to both protect herself and feed her hunger for attention. I saw the young woman whom as she bloomed did not know what genuine love was. She did not understand the power of her flower and thought a baby would give her all the love she desired. I saw the single mother strong and proud who struggled to raise three children with little help from their fathers who never could make ends meet, no matter how well she could make something out of nothing. The mother who begged the state for help only to have the doors of help and opportunity closed in her face. I saw her broken dreams, and the broken promises. And when my memories movie ended, I saw her face. Instead of my perfectly round face with high cheekbones and large expressive eyes, I saw the disfigured face of hurt. Tears began rolling down my deformed face. It was that moment when I knew what I had to do. I was not worth anything. I was a disgrace to my family, I could not hold on to a relationship or a job, and worst of all, my kids were suffering because of me.

"You wanted them taken away from me," I yelled at the mirror, "well you can have them!"

My children would not have to suffer from my failure anymore; I would take myself out of the equation. I opened the medicine cabinet where I had placed the filled steroid and pain pill bottles and I loosened the caps. As tears flowed down my face, I turned on the water and filled my hands.

"I love you babies," I said as I raised one bottle to my mouth.

A voice I was not expecting answered me back and stilled my movements.

"If you take your life who will take care of your children?" God said.

He spoke the only sentence that could stop me from taking my life. Why had He spoken? Why had He stopped me? Why would He not allow me to take myself away from all the pain and misery I felt? Why was He keeping me around?

I had to learn that God had a purpose for my life.

The Storm: Depression

"And do not lead us into temptation, but deliver us from [a]evil."
Matthew 6:13 (NASB)

Andrea Joyce

Sitting on the edge of my bed, a familiar voice from my past whispered sour nothings into my ears.

Moving back to Georgia had been an answered prayer from God. So much had happened in New Jersey, I was sorry I used it for an escape. The years in Georgia seemed a lot better than the years in New Jersey. Except, that I brought the old behaviors of New Jersey back with me. Though I had not taken my life, I had never resolved the negative emotions I had. When you do not deal with the negative emotions, pull them out from the root, and release them, they remain with you always able to sprout a new weed.

The first few years back in Georgia were good. I stayed with family before moving into my own place. The kids and I adjusted to our new life. The job I had suffered financial hardship, and they cut my hours. They asked me to work at the other business my supervisor owned, but without reliable transportation it all became too much. With less money coming in, I went back on the bill shuffle merry-go-round. Even though I had a certificate in Office Administrative Technology and experience in office assistant work, I only got hired for lower pay, bottom tier jobs. I was watching my peers make double and triple what I was making, and I felt the darkness of sadness welcome me home again. I was tired of trying to always find a way to meet all my expenses. Now I will not just blame not making enough, it took me a while to realize I was bad at managing the money I brought in. Over the years I had several jobs ranging from office management to administrative assisting. I knew working in the administrative field was temporary until I could find what I was interested in. A few years after graduating business school, there was nothing that held my attention. I worked for nursing homes, colleges, school systems, churches, corporate America, but nothing lasted very long. After a few years I would find some reason to leave, or the job would phase me out. It bothered me to not have the nice things I was used to having or living the lifestyle I had grown up with. I felt guilty that my children did not grow up the way I did. My parents took great care of us, and we never wanted for anything; we did not know lack or not having enough. There was never a time our lights were off, we did not have heat or food, or we were in danger of eviction or homelessness. Yet that was all my children knew and it made me feel like a failure.

One day after applying for jobs all morning, I sat on the side of my bed, looking out of the window. I had just received a call from the leasing office. They told me they had tried everything to hold off the inevitable, but they were going to have to file an eviction. I had lost my job three years before and had been working an at home customer service job barely making more than minimum wage. Friends, family, and organizations had helped me with rent those lean years, but their wells had run dry. There was nowhere else for me to go for help. I had exhausted my unemployment funds years before and had gone to the state agency for help, however once again there was no help for me. I tried to find ways to supplement my income and had worked several network marketing ventures, however selling was not my strong suit and I failed at them too. The car I had bought with a huge chunk of my income had turned out to be a lemon, leaving me once again without reliable transportation. As I sat on the bed musing, I heard a voice in my ear.

It said, "you're worthless. Why are you here taking up air? The kids would be better off without you."

When I heard those words, I cried. The voice was right, I was worthless. What value did I bring to my children, to my family, or myself? I looked around at the apartment I was about to lose and could not find one good thing that I was bringing to the table. In that moment I could only think of one thing to do, take myself out of the equation. This time the question "who would take care of your children if something happened to you" did not phase me. Hell, if I could not take care of them, anyone would be a better option. They were older now and would not need as much as they did when they were younger. They would be fine. I looked around my room focusing on the bathroom door. There were pain medications in the cabinet, but this time there would be no meds, it would be a blade. I wanted to leave swiftly. As I began planning, the enemy kept up his mantra in my ear.

"You're worthless, you're worthless."

Worthless... worthless. I had heard those words before. Hearing them transported me back to my seven-year relationship. The failed relationship that resulted into my rebound marriage. Though we were in a long relationship, it was not always a bed of roses. There were times he looked down on me because I had not graduated from college. I was in a relationship with a graduate of a prestigious Historically Black College and University (HBCU). He would make me feel like I was not on his level. I felt worthless. I thought about the jobs that did not pay enough because I did not have a degree, so even though I had experience and knowledge, I had to settle for lower pay. I felt worthless. Then I thought about me choosing men that were not consistent in their children's lives, again I felt worthless. I thought about not knowing what direction I wanted my life to go in. I felt worthless. I was stuck. Everything I had tried I failed at. I was worthless. The longer I sat on the bed, the louder the enemy's voice grew and the bigger my pity party became. I grew tired of rehearsing all my faults and failures; the deed needed to be done.

I walked into the kitchen I loved. The kitchen where I had cooked for my family and friends. I walked over to the dining room where we had many family dinners. I walked over to the living room and touched the couch, the first furniture that I had bought with my own money. I sat on the chaise part of the couch and looked around remembering the parties, meetings, and get-togethers I had hosted there over the last three years. It was bittersweet. I was losing the place that had held so much love and where I felt the most comfortable. However, I would not have to see the loss. I would not have to suffer the dreadful weight of the heavy knocks at the door when the marshals served the eviction notice, or the questioning eyes of the sheriff and crew putting our belongings and memories out on the street. Their eyes would speak their perplexity, and wonder what kind of mother I was. No, I wouldn't have to see them or see the disappointment in my kids' faces once again because we had lost another home. I had lost for the last time. This time no voice was going to stop me. There were no feelings of guilt. All I had was memories, like the one from seven years before. I had been in what I felt was a no-win situation and the only option I thought I had was to commit suicide. God's words stopped me and saved me. I was presently in a rough spot, but it was not as rough as the storm I faced seven years before. I thought, surely if God saved me back then with so much going against me, He could save me now.

I had to learn to remind myself that if God were able to help in the past, He could help in my present situation.

II. SEEING PAST THE STORM

SEEING PAST THE STORM

35 That day, at evening, Jesus said to his followers, "Come with me across the lake." 36 So they left the crowd behind and went with Jesus in the boat he was already in. There were also other boats that went with them. 37 A very bad wind came up on the lake. The waves were coming over the sides and into the boat, and it was almost full of water. 38 Jesus was inside the boat, sleeping with his head on a pillow. The followers went and woke him. They said, "Teacher, don't you care about us? We are going to drown!"

39 Jesus stood up and gave a command to the wind and the water. He said, "Quiet! Be still!" Then the wind stopped, and the lake became calm. Mark 4:35-39 (ERV)

Andrea Joyce

"Now to Him who is able to do far more abundantly beyond all that we ask or think, according to the power that works within us,"
Ephesians 3:20 (NASB)

Seeing Past Abandonment: Forgiveness

"Be kind to one another, compassionate, forgiving each other, just as God in Christ also has forgiven [a]you." Ephesians 4:32 (NASB)

I had to learn how to forgive.

Throughout my life from childhood to adulthood I harbored anger and bitterness towards my biological father. He was not the only one I held onto negative emotions for, however the most powerful emotions were against him. Instead of confronting the issues I had with him, I let them build up within me. The more time that lapsed the more negative emotions consumed me, first it was anger and bitterness. Hatred, resentment, rebelliousness, and disobedience soon followed. Jealousy and envy reared their ugly heads as did rage, self-loathing and promiscuity. The sad part was, besides hiding these emotions behind a mask to the world, I hid them from myself. I did not recognize that I had a problem. I was an angry child, an angrier teen, and an out-of-control young adult, but I thought it was normal to fly off the handle because someone canceled our date. I thought it was okay to put my hands on someone because they cheated on me. Normal to gun my engine and race over to a car intending to hit it because they had taken the parking space I was waiting for. These unacceptable behaviors were not normal, but they were mine for so many years I did not know how or who else to be. My anger and rage progressively got worse, and I could not control it. I did not know that the unforgiveness that I was carrying was the root of all the negative energy.

After my mother's constant encouragement, I called my father. I picked up the telephone, dialed his number and waited for him to answer. When he did, I told him I needed to speak to him, and he was fine with that.

"Hi dad," I said biting my lip.

"Hello Andrea, how are you?" he asked.

"I'm okay. I wanted to talk to you about something. It's kind of important."

"How much do you need?" he asked.

"I'm serious Dad," I said blowing out a breath of frustration.

"I am too. I don't have a lot to give you right now," he began.

"I am not calling about money. I want to get something off my chest," I replied.

"Okay. What's going on?"

"This is hard, but I wanted to be honest with you. I have been mad at you a long time. When you and Mommy broke up, you left me too. You said you would come see me, but you would not show up and it hurt my feelings. I was really angry with you," I said.

"Listen. I can't handle this right now. I don't want to talk about this," he said hanging up the phone.

Looking at the receiver as if it had bitten me, I could not believe that I had let down my guard, become vulnerable enough to express my bottled-up feelings and emotions and he had the nerve to tell me no. I vowed to never speak to him again. Meanwhile my negative emotions increased. Now my emotions were not just turned against me or him, but now the world had to feel my displeasure and discontent because I no longer cared about myself. I became even more reckless. I did not know what was causing me to feel the way I was or to do the things I was doing. I was twice divorced, raising three children and I was tired. I was tired of feeling these raw, negative emotions and not being able to control myself. I called my mother. As soon as she answered I broke into tears, and I confessed.

"Mom I do not want to feel like this anymore. I have no control of my feelings and I am tired of being angry. It consumes me. How do I stop these feelings?"

She told me to pray, and I almost hung up. I had been praying. By this time, I was a minister, spreading the Word of God, I prayed all the time. My mother would not let me off easy. She told me to pray specifically for God to help me overcome my anger and then she said the very thing she had been saying for years.

"But first you must pray and ask God to help you forgive your father."

Her words echoed in my ears countless times throughout my life, but this time I listened. I asked if that would help me defeat the anger and she told me it was a necessary step. I told her I had tried to forgive many times, but it never worked. She shared her insight with me.

"When you want to forgive from your heart, when you really mean it, God will help you forgive. Just keep asking Him to help you."

As we were hanging up, she told me she would pray too because she wanted me to be released from all the negativities. I would like to say that the first time I prayed God delivered me from unforgiveness, however it would be another two years before it happened. While I waited to be released from it, I began calling my father. I would ball my fists up and dial his number while gritting my teeth, praying he would not answer, so I could just leave a message. When he would answer even though I would not have much to say, I would try to have a normal conversation. I would talk about what was happening in my life and the lives of my children. I would tell him what was happening in Atlanta and ask him what he had going on in New Jersey. At the end of each call, I would make a face as he told me he loved me, and I would respond in kind.

I was in a group at my church that helped us to deal with our past hurts and pains. It was in this group where I could release all my feelings towards my father. There was an exercise where we had to write a letter to the person who caused us the most pain. Writing the letter was our homework and at the next meeting we had to read the letter aloud. As the words on the page flowed through my lips, I felt the ease in my stance as the weight rose from my shoulders. The words that gave life to my feelings were released and even though I cried, I was no longer sad or angry. It was a few weeks later that I felt a peace come over me. When I thought of my father, I did not get angry or frustrated as I had before reading the letter. When I heard his name or spoke about him, I no longer clenched my fist, glared, or frowned. I knew I had forgiven my father. The test of that forgiveness came a few months later when he had both a stroke and his first heart attack. I was so glad that God had freed me from the bondage of unforgiveness because I would have missed being there for him. We became closer and talked a few times a month. I also visited him a few times. I won't say that we had the best father-daughter relationship out there because by the time the forgiveness had happened, I had fallen in love with the dad that had raised me and he had taken the first spot in my heart. But my biological father and I would talk more frequently, and he was a better grandfather to my children than he was a father to me, and I appreciated that. It helped when several years later he passed away and I felt no guilt because I had let everything go. My mother had often said that I would carry guilt if something were to happen to him and I had not forgiven him. I'm glad that I never had to test that out.

Forgiving my father was the necessary action I needed for other things in my life to go right. Holding onto all those negative emotions made my life unbearable and almost unlivable. The choices I made stemmed from the hurt feelings and because of my hurt, I hurt others. I had to overcome my issues with my father so I could work on having a healthy life and healthy relationships with my family and friends. It is easier for me to forgive others because I learned to forgive him.

Andrea Joyce

Seeing Past Rejection: Loving Myself

"He who gets [a]wisdom loves his own soul;
He who keeps understanding will find good." Proverbs 19:8 (NKJV)

I needed to learn how to love the skin I was in.

Loving my skin tone happened by accident. I was in my 30s when my children and I were invited to an event. I was excited to go and realized I did not have a cute shirt to wear. I only had business clothes, church clothes and sweats, nothing in between so we went shopping. In the store, I headed for my usual choice, dark colors. My oldest daughter stopped me and held up a bright pink shirt suggesting I get it because it would look good on me. I refused and moved past her to look at black tops. She persisted and held up the shirt again and insisted I wear it. I told her in no uncertain terms that I would not be purchasing that shirt. There was a shift in our relationship that day because she refused to listen to me, and I wondered who the parent and who the child was. After going back and forth for several moments I got the black top. Unbeknownst to me she purchased the pink top she wanted me to wear so badly. When we began getting ready for the event, I could not find my new black top. It was nearing time for the event to start, and I was in a panic because I could not find my shirt. My daughter came into the room holding up the pink shirt and I think I turned into a madwoman. I started yelling and crying about her forcing me to wear that bright shirt. I had a meltdown right in front of her. Over the years I had become so programmed not to wear bright colors I could not make myself do it. After my 20-minute tantrum I yanked the shirt on mad at her and the world and stormed out to the car.

In the car my youngest daughter asked me what was wrong, and I burst into tears. I tried to explain what I went through growing up with my complexion and the mean comments. I was conditioned not to wear bright colors, and I was having a panic attack because I was wearing pink. After I calmed down, we went to the event and the craziest thing happened, I received compliments at every turn. People came up to me smiling saying I was beautiful. Others said that I was glowing, and pink looked great on me. I was getting so much attention I went to my oldest daughter and asked if she had paid people to come up to me. She promised she had not, she looked into my eyes and said that I was getting the attention because I looked good in the color. When we returned home, I looked at myself, I mean really looked at myself and looked for the girl that had been teased, the girl that tried to scrape and bleach the darkness off her, the one who had been talked about, but I did not see her. I saw a pretty girl who looked great in pink. Her dark skin glowed in that pink shirt and as I realized she was me, tears of healing flowed. From that time on, I started experimenting with other bright colors and discovered that green was not my favorite color anymore, yellow became the color I loved. I started walking into the complexion that I hid from and realized that my black was beautiful. God made me and because of that I made it a point to love the skin I was in.

Seeing Past Violation: Protection

"My God, my rock, in whom I take refuge, my shield, and the horn of my salvation, my stronghold and my refuge, my savior; you save me from violence. I call upon the Lord, who is worthy to be praised, and I am saved from my enemies." Psalm 26:1 (ESV)

I had to learn how to release guilt and shame. I had to learn that the events were not my fault, and I needed to forgive myself.

It took me a long time to move past the near rape that happened to me at college. I was dealing with a double violation, one done physically and the other done emotionally. My former friend had taken a part of me I could never bring back, my virtue. No, I was not a virgin, but I had a belief about sex, it was to be shared, given, not taken. How could someone take something that belongs to another even after they say no? He stole my soul, my very essence. I would never be the same. My boyfriend had taken a part of me that took years for me to regain. He took away my belief in all men. I always believed that your significant other would always have your back, no matter what. It is what I was raised to believe. Couples took care of each other; they did not accuse each other.

It was over 15 years later that I could finally say no to the questions that plagued me surrounding my near rape. It was not until I wrote a paper about my incident that I could even admit something happened to me. When I wrote it, I analyzed what happened. I blamed myself. What man would want a woman who went through that? I thought. I was damaged goods, and I felt guilty because I was not strong enough to fight back. I was ashamed that I trusted someone who could hurt me like that. I thought I had good instincts about people, yet I let a wolf into my life. The incident had crippled me emotionally, physically, and mentally. I did not share with anyone what happened, and I would become ice cold and tremble if anyone talked about rape or molestation. I thought if I didn't think about it or talk about it, it would go away. It changed me. I shrank away from physical contact, then I found myself not caring if I was touched. I became hot and cold. There were days I would sit in a ball on the bed crying and other days I was carefree.

After I wrote the paper, I thought I would be okay. I thought I had gotten the incident out of my system, and all was well. All was well until the night I hung out with some friends. We went to a lounge to have some fun. When we arrived a mutual friend of ours was outside waiting. I had known this man for at least a year, and we always had fun with him. This night he had forgone his usual GQ look and instead wore jeans, a button up, and a baseball hat. His dressed down appearance was not the issue. When he turned to greet me, I dropped to the ground and began hyperventilating. I was looking into the face of my near rapist. I had never realized how much he favored the man who had violated me. My former friend had always wore jeans, a button-up shirt and a baseball hat. They had the same face shape and the same brown complexion. I was transported back to that room fighting to keep from being raped. My friends did not understand what was happening and rushed over to calm me down. I could not calm down; I could not shake off that monster's face looking down at me tightening his grip around my throat and fighting to pull my jeans off. It would take hours before I could get myself together and realize that our acquaintance was not the same man. It was then that I knew I needed help.

I began talking to God. God helped me to forgive my father, now I needed His help to release the trauma I experienced. I wrote and spoke more about my experience. The more I shared the more I healed. I also talked to the boyfriend I had been dating during that situation. We talked everything out and got closure. As I began thinking about the incident, I became grateful. Grateful because not everyone has the same story of being able to walk away without fully being violated. I was also grateful for God's protection. Yes, something bad happened, however when I think about his hand taking my breath away, the darkness of death surrounding me and him being obsessed with penetrating me no matter what, I was grateful that he did not kill me, that he did not rape me and even though I was traumatized for years, I could tell me story and get the healing I needed. The healing process took years and continues today.

Seeing Past Heartbreak: Healing

"Behold, I will bring to it health and healing, and I will heal them and reveal to them abundance of prosperity and security. " Jeremiah 33:6 (ESV)

I needed to learn how to heal.

One of my biggest regrets was not knowing how to forgive. I held onto grudges for years and burned many bridges because of my unwillingness to forgive. Not only did I not know how to forgive, but I also knew nothing about how to heal from emotional wounds. Instead of dealing with hurt I just pushed it down and moved on to the next thing or the next person, ignoring the pain I felt. I set a dangerous pattern for my life. Because I did not deal with hurt and pain it spilled over into other relationships and the men, I dated did not get a fair chance with me. As soon as they did anything wrong, I was ready to cut them off, or I shut down. They never fully got my heart, no matter how hard they tried.

After one of the break ups, God sat me down. He took dating away from me. I could not get a date if I paid for it. Anytime anyone would show any interest in me they would disappear. It became common to hear "I don't know what happened. One day we were talking and then you disappeared." At first it was a joke to me. Okay no dates for a month or two that was fine, when two months turned into six months and then a year it stopped being funny. I was accustomed to having a male companion, so to go from constant companionship to none at all sent me into a loneliness pitfall. After the second year of not dating, I had a come to Jesus meeting and wanted to know what was going on. It was placed in my spirit that since the age of 17 I had not been alone; I had not had time to heal from any relationship I had been in. So, the year before and that year I was in the midst of healing. I told God that I appreciated the time of healing, but I was ready to get back in the dating game. I know I amused God; I am pretty sure he had a pleasant laugh at that because my next relationship happened almost 9 years later.

During those years, I had time to assess my past relationships. I wrote the pros and cons of each attachment also confessing my true feelings for each one. I learned a lot about myself. Besides my fiancé and two of the connections, I had not been friends with anyone I had dated. It was either a physical connection or a rebound relationship. I had not really liked them because I did not really know them or given myself a chance to get to know them. Every few years I do assessments of my relationships to see what else I can learn.

I realized that one of the biggest areas that needed to be healed, was me learning who I was. Every time I dated someone I would change. There would be a change in the beginning. I would try to embody who they thought I was or thought I should be and pick up some of their likes and dislikes. There was a change when things ended. I became more jaded, more bitter. Picking up their behaviors had me not knowing who I was anymore. I did not know what I liked. I lost myself in the relationships. After analyzing my relationships, my next step was to analyze me. I had to examine myself and see who I was and if I liked what I saw. I took a deep look inside myself and rediscovered myself. For healing to work there needs to be complete honesty and a willingness to put in work. I made the commitment to heal. I have begun caring for myself daily, checking in with my emotions and feelings. In the mornings I read a scripture verse and I meditate and pray throughout the day. I have also begun journaling so I can talk about what happened throughout the day. Healing is a continuous journey.

Seeing Past Betrayal: Loyalty

"One who has unreliable friends soon comes to ruin,
   but there is a friend who sticks closer than a brother." Proverbs 18:24 (NIV)

I had to learn that not everyone who shouted friend was a friend.

Matthew 22:39 says, "Love your neighbor the same as you love yourself." (ESV) The problem with that scripture is that if you do not love yourself, it will be hard for you to love others. Because I was harboring negative emotions, I was attracting people who had issues going on as well. The people we attract mirror who we are.

I always blamed others for the things I went through. I never looked at myself and accepted my fault in things. That lack of responsibility kept me pointing at others instead of pointing at me, the one who needed repairing. As friendships ended, I picked up more feelings of hurt, resentment, anger, and bitterness. I never dealt with my feelings. I pretended breakups did not affect me and I was unbothered and unconcerned by lost friendships, when in fact I was hurt to my core.

As I examined myself, I realized I was a people pleaser. I was someone that needed to make people happy even at the expense of my own happiness. As much as I rebelled and tried to be hard, I looked for people's validation. I wanted to be accepted, to belong, and I wanted to be included, so I allowed things to go on that were not right. Red flags and unacceptable behaviors were ignored just to make others happy.

I learned there are only two people you should consider pleasing, God and yourself. Sacrificing yourself for others leads some to think you are a doormat and your feelings do not matter. When you do not prioritize yourself, you have feelings of resentment toward others. We understand that loving, helping, and giving to others is important, however if your tank is empty, you will have nothing to give to anyone else. When you live for others, you sacrifice your needs and wants, and you might be in jeopardy of disobeying God. Let me give you an example. You just taught a powerful lesson during bible study. There were people there that heard the lesson, came up to you afterwards and said they had been struggling with the street life and coming back to church, but because of what God spoke through you they were going to turn their lives around and start coming to church. You are tired. You know you should go home, bathe and recuperate from the events of that day. Instead of doing what you feel in your spirit, you decide to accept the invitation from your friend to go clubbing because they have no one else to go with and they do not want to go by themselves. You hear a voice telling you to go home, you do, but it is just to change into an outfit more suitable for the club than the pulpit. You walk into the club shaking your money maker and walk right into the same people you had just ministered to a few hours before. They give you a hurt, disgusted look and you never see them in church again. That was my testimony, and I carried guilt a long time for turning people away from God by my actions. Sometimes pleasing God and you means telling people no, sometimes it means losing friendships and family. When you put God first, a lot of things and people fall into place or out of your life.

When I began assessing myself, I began praying and asking God to reveal to me who people were in my life. Who were the reason people? The people in my life because something needed to be accomplished and after it was finished their time was up. Who were the season people? These were the people who were temporary, who were just there for that period and stage of my life. And who were the lifetime people? Who was supposed to be in my life forever? Those were not my only questions to Him. I also wanted to know how to categorize people. Who were the friends, the acquaintances, the assignments, the associates, the distractions, and the pretenders? I wanted to know who people were so I would know how to deal with them. I also used this prayer for males I was interested in. After all the years of poor decisions, I wanted to know from the beginning, who I needed to leave alone. I had chosen wrong before. I had picked out wedding dresses for men who were only an assignment and I had tossed away men that were supposed to be in my life for a lifetime. God is faithful, He gave me signs. I had to learn to listen to Him and move when He said move. He is the most loyal friend I have ever had, I needed to be loyal to Him and his infinite wisdom.

Andrea Joyce

Seeing Past Homelessness: Releasing Pride

"When pride comes, then comes dishonor;
But with the humble there is wisdom." Proverbs 11:2 (NASB)

I had to learn how to let go of pride and ask for help.

One of my biggest reasons for not forgiving was not because I did not know how, it was because I did not want to let go. I did not want to let my guard down and admit that they hurt me. I was uncomfortable being vulnerable. Being vulnerable with a person was knowing they had the power to hurt me and giving them the opportunity to do it. I was a part of the "never let them see you hurt" mindset. Holding on to this mindset allowed pride to fester within me. We are not talking about the pride that means being satisfied with an accomplishment, but the pride that is a puffed-up ego.

This pride that was growing within me told me I did not need anyone. It told me that if I showed any weakness people would talk about me, laugh at me, and judge me. This negative emotion settled right in with the unforgiveness, bitterness, resentment, anger, low self-esteem, and the other negativity I housed. I did not like asking for help because it made me feel weak and I thought weakness was a bad thing. I also did not want to ask for help because I did not want the hurt feelings from being told no. After hearing "no" several times when I was in dire situations it was a feeling, I did not want to suffer through. I figured with my high intellect and cunning, I could figure my way out of anything. How wrong I was.

My mother would tell me not to do something that was meant to hurt someone else that would ultimately hurt me too. I did not listen. Sometimes just letting go of my pride would have eased bad things from happening, but I held onto it with a steel grip. As I held on to that pride, I watched blessings slip away. While pride comforted me, solutions to my problems faded away. The more I failed and the more I lost out, the tighter I held onto my pride. I was already angry about other things, now I turned that anger towards people that should have known I needed help but did not offer it. No, I did not ask, I just assumed they should know.

"Why don't they call me and see if I need anything? They know I am raising three kids by myself with no child support."

I held on to that bitterness and misplaced anger. James 4:2 says, "You do not have because you do not ask" (NASB). To preserve my pride, I did not ask, and I lost out. Living in the van showed me it was not just my life that would suffer because of my pride, my children would suffer too. As a parent, the last thing I wanted was for my children to struggle because of me. It took a while, but I began being open and honest with people when I needed help. I had to work on not asking at the last minute, but I began asking. I understood there were times people would be unable or unwilling to help me and it was not meant to be taken as rejection. When I examined myself, I discovered that when people told me no, I felt a sense of rejection, that's why it hurt me. Even though it was different people, it always brought me back to that little girl whose father had abandoned her and whose crush had rejected her. Even though it was a new pain, I was rehearsing an old wound. In order for me to remove pride, I would also have to remove those feelings of rejection and abandonment.

Seeing Past Addiction: Dependence

"Trust ye in the Lord for ever: for in the Lord Jehovah is everlasting strength:" Isaiah 26:4 (KJV)

I had to learn to stop relying on crutches.

I relied on the candy, the same way I relied on the alcohol. They were crutches to help me get through troublesome times. While they were being used as crutches, my body began craving them physically. I depended on alcohol and the mint to help me forget what I had been through and what I was going through. The alcohol was a little different because once the negative situation was removed, I could stop drinking. I could not do that with the mint as easily.

Physically I could say my body was hooked to the sugar, but it went deeper than that. Even though my circumstance changed, my mindset had not. I depended on those candies for stability. They were the only stable thing in my life. When I could not find the mint for almost a week, I went into a state of panic, not just because my body had become accustomed to it, but also because my crutch had been taken away and I was not ready to deal with reality and stand on my own.

I had lost my place and even though I had been blessed to move somewhere else, there was no guarantee that homelessness would not happen again. That was my fear, that was my worry, and the mint was my comfort zone. I could look past my fear, worry, and doubt and focus on it always being there for me.

I had to ween myself off the candy and lean on God. I had to relearn how to trust Him. When I gave my life to Jesus completely, I thought nothing bad would happen to me ever again. I had first accepted Christ at 16, but I did not know what I was doing. A group of my friends decided to do it all together one Sunday morning at church. All I knew were bible stories and some scriptures from Sunday school. I did not know God for real. I thought He was a mean spirit that sent everyone to hell. If you did anything wrong to hell you would go, since I knew I did a lot of bad things I thought I knew where I was headed when I died. I only knew two prayers growing up, "The Lord's Prayer" and "Now I Lay Me Down to Sleep". I did not know that prayer was a dialogue between you and God, a conversation from your heart and His. I did not know you could actually talk to Him, I thought you had to go to the priest and then the priest would talk to Him on your behalf. Understand I was raised in the African Methodist Episcopal Church and attended Catholic school. I was rooted in two different doctrines, and I was confused. When I decided to become a Christian and give my life to Christ, I went with my friends to the front of the church an early Sunday morning I did not know what I was doing. I did not know what being a follower of Jesus really meant, I was did what my friends and I had agreed to do. Years later I would begin learning more about God and having a relationship with him when I attended a Baptist church. I learned more about Him, but still did not learn how to talk to Him. I began reading my Bible trying to find answers but except for the Bible stories I had read when I was a child, I did not understand what the King James Bible was saying.

It would be another 5 years before I understood what having a relationship with God was. Attending my first nondenominational church taught me the foundation of Christianity and allowed me to open my heart and accept God into my life earnestly. I learned how to pray, I read different versions of the Bible so I could understand it and one day King James even made sense. With me walking closer with God and having a genuine relationship with Him, I could not understand how bad things were still happening to me. I thought maybe before truly accepting Christ into my life things were bad because I was not fully joined to Him, so surely when I said "I Do" to Him my life would be a bed of roses. Not so, if anything it seemed harder. It seemed like attacks and storms were coming from every direction. I used a tool I had learned to help me through tough situations. Faith. Faith is believing even when you don't see a way, or it makes little sense. I had to have the faith to believe that God was going to rescue me from the storm like He did the disciples in Matthew 8:23-27. I had to depend on Him, not my crutch, for my next steps. Throughout my life in rough situations when I wanted to give up, my mother would ask, "where is your faith?" I never fully understood it until all I had was God. When my family could not help me, when friends turned their backs on me, when doctor reports were negative and when my housing and jobs came into question, all I could do was give all those doubts, worries and fears to God in prayer and trust that He would handle every situation.

Seeing Past Suicide: Purpose

"The Lord will perfect that which concerneth me: thy mercy, O Lord, endureth for ever: forsake not the works of thine own hands." Psalm 138:8 (KJV)

I had to learn that God had a purpose for my life.

When I lifted the pill bottle and began pouring out the pills that would end my life, I heard a voice say, "If you take your life who will take care of your children." That question halted my actions and fresh tears rolled down my face. My children, my three heartbeats. The innocent little people who had not asked to be born or to be living through my situations. All they knew was me, their fathers had walked out of their lives. I was on the outs with other family members, so I could not be sure that they would love and care for my children in my absence. I had not kept in touch with either of the paternal sides of my family, so I was not sure they could or would help. With those thoughts in mind, I knew I had to stay alive. There was no way I was going to allow my children to go through the foster care system instead I flushed the pills down the toilet.

Since so much was going wrong in my life, I called on God to help me. I was not sure how I was going to overcome everything, but since He talked me into staying, I knew He had to have a plan for me. I needed to know what the purpose was for my life. At 15, I heard a voice call my name and tell me I would be a minister. I looked all over but my parents were not home, so it was not them and my brother was only 8, his voice was nowhere as deep as the voice I heard. I told God "no" to the calling of being a minister. I ran from that calling until I was 33. It was then that I began the training and education necessary to become a minister. I taught and preached the Word of God; I knew there was more.

To balance the negative situations, I tried to make the kids' lives fun. I took my oldest to an audition for a play my friend was directing, and she booked the role. We now had something positive to focus on. Things were going well until rehearsals began. The place that was used for rehearsals had a terrible vibe. Whenever we went there, I would feel like I was being choked have severe headaches, and my spirit was uneasy. My daughter felt the same way. While sitting amid the negative vibes I prayed and asked God to send a playwright that would listen to Him and not use just any place, but keep the kids secure and safe from all manners of negative spirits. After I prayed my eloquent prayer, God spoke to me. I was not used to Him answering so quickly and when He gave me the answer, I wished I had not prayed. He told me since I had the issue, I was the solution. He told me to write a play that my daughter could act in. Just like with the minister's calling, I told God no. There was no way I could write a play. I had never written a play; I was not even sure how to set up the script template. He would not back down or let it go, I reluctantly agreed. Before I would go forward, I asked that three conditions be met. I asked first that He help me write the play. Second, that anyone who touched my production would be blessed holistically and third that even if it be one person, that people would be saved because of the play. I began writing the play while I was homeless. I spent some of those times in the park writing it. After my suicide contemplation, I went back to writing it and completed it in 2008. That play would be the beginning of me walking into owning my production company. I wrote more scripts and screenplays. God showed me that writing was one of my callings and He showed me that speaking was another one. I have been gifted with various talents and skills, but I would not have known them if I had taken my life that sorrowful day.

There are times we end things too early because we do not see any fruit from our hard work and struggles. We might not be bearing fruit because a pruning needs to happen, some things, habits, and people may need to be cut out of our lives so we can be prosperous. We might not be bearing fruit because we are planted in the wrong field. Sometimes we might not bear fruit because we give up working, tilling, and watering the soil because it seems like too much work, and it takes too long. We see others bearing fruit and get frustrated with our lack of production and we give up. You will never know how close to the breakthrough you are until you reach it.

Andrea Joyce

Seeing Past Depression: Promise

"And my God will supply every need of yours according to his riches in glory in Christ Jesus." Philippians 4:19 (ESV)

I had to learn to remind myself that if God was able to help in the past, He could help in my present situation.

As I sat on the couch thinking about the last time I had been in a dire situation, I was reminded of God's voice telling me that my children would have no one if I took my life. I remembered how I flushed the pills, cried, and walked away from that cry for help. I remembered how He began blessing me; Unemployment was granted, the state began helping me with food, my mother and I had reconciled, she had even blessed me with a vehicle, and I had become closer to God and began preaching and teaching His Word like never before. Even as things still were not perfect, they were better. I discovered my callings, some of them anyway. I remembered conversations with God, and some things He had promised me. I knew God was not a liar, so if He promised something, unlike my earthly biological father, it had to come to pass. I had not walked into the promises of God, so how was I going to take my life before I fulfilled them. His promises to me were not my promises alone. He had promised some things for my children, my great-grandchildren, my legacy. If I took myself out, I would cancel out their promises, their future. My life was not just about me, it was about others.

I remembered the words my loving dad spoke.

"Your life is a part of a bigger picture. Your decisions do not just affect you they affect everyone in your life and even people you may not know. Stop looking at that small area that's in your face, take a step back, and look at the complete picture before you make a decision."

If God's promises for my family and those He called me to were going to come through me, I needed to be there to walk into them. It was not until I had this revelation that God spoke to me. He restated His promises and who He called me to be. He did not coddle me but told me to get to work and that the spirit of suicide had been broken off me and my bloodline.

Even though I have had some down moments and gone through a few depressions, I never revisited my suicidal thoughts. I know God will work out any situation and storm I face, no matter how much it hurts and no matter how many losses I take. God will ultimately give me the victory.

III. THE BLESSING IN THE STORM

Andrea Joyce

The Blessing in the Storm

"When you pass through the waters, I will be with you; and through the rivers, they shall not overwhelm you; when you walk through fire you shall not be burned, and the flame shall not consume you." Isaiah 43:2 (ESV)

The Blessing

The three things I needed to help me overcome some of the storms of my life were God's mercy, time, and forgiveness. Even though it did not feel like it at the time, there was a blessing in each of those storms that helped strengthen me and become more reliant on God. I can honestly say my relationship with Him is better because of the storms. There was a point in time when I relied on myself only. I had been through so much disappointment and heartache depending on others I did not trust anyone but me. The storms showed me I was not strong enough by myself to defeat them. I needed someone else but not just anyone, I needed God. Through God, people were sent to me that loved me past my trauma, hurt, and pain. He sent me prayer warriors that taught me not only how to pray for myself but how to pray for others even when I was at rock bottom. I was able to reconcile my past self with my present self and work on building up a better me. I learned to talk to God, to share my hurts, pains, thoughts, and ideas with Him. More importantly I learned to listen. I will not say that I always listen, I'm still a little hardheaded, but I listen more. I take time to meditate so I can center myself and my emotions. I do not do it every day, but if I feel stressed or overwhelmed, I take a few minutes to focus on my breathing or concentrate on a scripture. I still get angry at times; however, I also try to look at the big picture and all that I have to lose. I allow myself to have the feelings, but I do not stay there. Communication helps to release me from negative emotions. I try to speak to the source, if I cannot, then I talk to God, another trusted friend or I write it out. I have learned to forgive. It is not always easy and sometimes it takes a while, but I let go of grudges before they can fester. Even though I forgive, I do not always restore relationships. If there is negativity and toxicity, I let it go. You do not have to allow harmful behavior and poisonous people in your life. There are several things I am still working on, vulnerability and letting my walls down is one, a big one. Working on becoming your best self is a daily process; it is never ending.

In the storm you see who people are, yourself included. You lose some people; you may gain others. God is constant, He's always there. We can continue striking out on our own or we can turn to Him for help, direction, and guidance. The choice is ours. Though we walk away from God time and time again, He waits right there in that last place where we left Him, with open arms. Waiting for an invitation to come into the situation and correct it. If you are going through a storm, a struggle, or an adverse situation, turn back to Him, ask Him to forgive you for whatever you've done, ask Him to help you forgive others and yourself, and then invite Him in to work out the situation and let Him do it in His timing and in His own way. It might not be when you want it to happen and it might not happen the way you want it to, but when God handles a situation, it is handled for your good and His glory.

"If my people, which are called by my name, shall humble themselves, and pray, and seek my face, and turn from their wicked ways; then will I hear from heaven, and will forgive their sin, and will heal their land." 2 Chronicles 7:14 (KJV)

If you have not received Jesus Christ into your life as your Lord and Savior and you would like to do so, please pray this prayer with me. "With my mouth I confess and admit that I am a sinner. I believe Jesus is the Son of God and was sent to die for my sins. I accept Him as my Savior, and I pledge my life to following Him." If you have prayed this prayer and believe it in your heart, you have just been saved. Welcome into the Body of Christ! Please find a Bible based, Bible teaching church in your local community where they can help you continue your journey as a believer. If you need any additional information or for prayer, please email withministries1@gmail.com and one of the dedicated staff will assist you.

"9 That if thou shalt confess with thy mouth the Lord Jesus, and shalt believe in thine heart that God hath raised him from the dead, thou shalt be saved.

10 For with the heart man believeth unto righteousness; and with the mouth confession is made unto salvation." Romans 10:9-10 (KJV)

"9 that if you confess with your mouth the Lord Jesus and believe in your heart that God has raised Him from the dead, you will be saved. 10 For with the heart one believes unto righteousness, and with the mouth confession is made unto salvation." Romans 10:9-10 (NKJV)

"9 If you declare with your mouth, "Jesus is Lord," and believe in your heart that God raised him from the dead, you will be saved. 10 For it is with your heart that you believe and are justified, and it is with your mouth that you profess your faith and are saved." Romans 10:9-10 (NIV)

Andrea Joyce

IV. WORDS FROM THE AUTHOR

Thank you so much for purchasing this book. In these pages you will read about my personal struggles, storms, and challenges. You will read about my tests and my ultimate testimonies, the victories I had through God. I hope within these pages you find peace and strength to get through what you are facing. Remember there is nothing we cannot do with God on our side. May He bless you through your trials and tribulations. I pray for success and victory for you!

Andrea Joyce

ABOUT THE AUTHOR

Andrea Joyce's debut book "31 Ways to Self-Care" fulfilled her goal of helping those who feel burdened and hopeless. Raised in Paterson, New Jersey Andrea Joyce is no stranger to adversity, writing her first stage play as a mechanism to change her life. Prepared to chart her own path, Andrea Joyce moved to Atlanta, Georgia putting her mark on the entertainment field establishing two production companies. The mother of three extraordinary humans, her most cherished title is Mom. Andrea Joyce is also a Certified Life Coach, Minister, Playwright, Director and Producer. In her spare time, Andrea, as known by family and friends enjoys traveling and fine dining.

Visit her online at www.authorandreajoyce.com
You may contact her at:
Instagram: @AuthorAndreaJoyce
Facebook: @Author Andrea Joyce
Email: authorandreajoyce@gmail.com

Made in the USA
Middletown, DE
09 February 2025